Innuendo Bonanza!

GARRY BUSHELL

Copyright © 2015 Garry Bushell

All rights reserved.

ISBN-13: 978-1514866290

Garry Bushell has asserted his right under the Copyright, Designs and Patents Act 1998 to be identified as the author of this work.

CONDITIONS OF SALE

All rights reserved. No part of this publication may be reproduced, stored in a retrieval system, or transmitted in any form or by any means, electronic, mechanical, photocopying, scanning, recording or otherwise without the prior permission of the publisher.

This book has been sold subject to the condition that it shall not, by way of trade or otherwise, be lent, resold, hired out or otherwise circulated without the publisher's prior consent in any form or binding or cover other than that in which it is published and without a similar condition including this condition being imposed on the subsequent purchaser.

Published in Great Britain by Litopia® in association with Garry Bushell Enterprises Ltd

"Litopia" is a registered trade mark.

First edition July 2015

About Garry

Son of a fireman, Garry trained under the legendary Paul Foot on the *Socialist Worker* – and was promptly placed under surveillance by the British security services.

They're probably still watching him.

As show business editor of *The Sun*, he became in Ross Kemp's words, "the most feared critic in the business". He's written best-selling biographies and two gripping crime novels, and he is deeply associated with British youth cults, rock, punk and Ska bands.

Garry has discovered new talent by the bucket-load, managed bands, championed working class comics and notched up a Number One hit. His #1 rated ITV series *Bushell On The Box* trounced *Coronation Street* for audience share.

Foreword

To err is human; to really cock things up, you need a TV presenter.

There isn't a breakfast telly personality in the world who hasn't put their foot in their mouth at least once in their career – and the same goes for sports commentators, weather forecasters and wittering celebrities.

I started collecting 'Garry's Goofs' more than 20 years ago, in 1987, when my 'Bushell on the Box' column was first published in The Sun. Since then it has appeared in the *Daily Star*, *The People* and the *Daily Star Sunday*.

My readers have always seemed to enjoy sending in clangers. (Newspaper editors must love Garry's Goofs too, as several of them currently run blatant copies of the feature without so much as a thank you – let alone a royalty cheque.) Being easily amused, those that appeal to me most are the saucy innuendoes – although this collection does include other howlers, mostly from live presenters and commentators who tend, by the very nature of their jobs, to talk first and think later.

Some of these characters are now lost in the mists of time. How many of us remember TV-am's Kathy Taylor, who welcomed Frank Sinatra as 'Hank', called Trudie Styler 'Judy' and introduced Star Trek's William Shatner as 'Captain Kirk of Star Check fame'?

I particularly miss Ulrika Jonsson, whose daily TVAM weather forecasts could be relied upon to deliver regular morning glories. She had more goofs than husbands – and many of them are recalled in this volume. Thankfully, her successors – such as Fiona Phillips and Lorraine Kelly – have managed to continue their impressive strike rate of cock-ups. And it's hard to forget Eamonn Holmes startling Fiona by asking, "Would you spread your legs for this?" (Mercifully, he was talking about a dance video.)

Luckily for me TV presenters still get it gloriously wrong. Earlier this year, BBC South Today's Sally Taylor managed to refer live on air to the famous writer Hilaire Belloc as "Hilaire Bollock." That's what I call dropping a Belloc...

Once you start looking for goofs, you find them everywhere. I was in Southend when I noticed a sign by the side of a Portaloo which seemed to be inviting passers-by to 'Stop and drain cock,' while a recent headline from the AOL homepage boldly alerted me to the case of the 'Police Chief Tossed In Jail.' (The lucky swine!)

An advert in the 'Pets Corner' of the *Bury Journal* boasted: "Village Studios – have your pet shot professionally," and I once noticed this sign on a huge electrical generator, gravely warning passers-by: 'DANGER! To touch these wires will result in instant death – anyone found doing it will be severely prosecuted.'

(Quite right too; even if they'd have to scrape them into a bucket first.)

Naturally, newspapers aren't immune. Who could forget the classic headlines 'Man Found Dead In Graveyard' or 'Women's Chorus Adds Belcher To Membership'? The latter was about a lady going under the name of Laura Belcher. I particularly liked the newspaper headline about redundancies which screamed: '100 Blow Jobs'.

TV presenter Jay Leno in the USA revels in finding newspaper misprints, like the bath product advert which innocently asked, "What's better than a hot bath with your rubber dickie?' and he also discovered 'Vagina Ham' on offer on a US menu. (It's safe to assume that they'd meant Virginia – unless Heidi Fleiss has moved into the catering business.) Thanks to Jay we learn that California had a Big Wang restaurant, and that a New York beauty salon was naively offering a "quick hand job" along with their more time-consuming manicures.

US papers like to use the names of couples marrying hyphenated together in their wedding page announcements, which has resulted in such dream duos as Whyde-Hole, Godown-Gross, Hogg-Paradise, Seaman-Sample, Toole-Burns, Johnson-Whacker, Cockman-Dickeman, Annis-Biter and the all-time classic Butts-Fudger. And what man wouldn't have felt a tremor of fear in reading the words, 'Wang-Crumpler to Wed'?

But written clangers are no substitute for verbal ones, and

this is where TV comes into its own. David Coleman is Britain's most notorious offender. His frequent bloopers were dubbed 'Colemanballs' by *Private Eye*, the former satirical magazine, after he came out with comments like this one from a race at the 1976 Olympics: "The big Cuban opened his legs and showed his class."

So what is the difference between a Colemanball and a classic Garry's Goof? Simple: it's all in the mind, or, more precisely, the filthy minds of the great British public. Colemanballs are experts talking gibberish. Garry's Goofs are rooted in the traditional English love of the innuendo, in particular the unintentional double meaning. So while Phil Thompson informing us that "Giles Barnes needs to be a bit more cleverer" is a Colemanball, Matt Chilton's remark while covering the women's luge on Eurosport, that "Anna Orlava is sloppy in the thrust chute, good at the right-hander," is unmistakably a Garry's Goof.

See also Kate Humble's "adorable beaver", every female weightlifter's snatch and any sporting commentary that involved, "Matthew Pinsent rolling around, enjoying a nice length" (© Garry Herbert).

I make no apology for the fact that most of my goofs are vulgar, lowbrow and unlikely to appeal to the snobs of Eggleston Hall (on ITV's *Ladettes to Ladies*). Like most people raised on *Carry On* films and *The Benny Hill Show*, I relish this sort of traditional English sauce. Its roots go right back to Chaucer and it flourished in our grandparents' days in the comedy patter of Max Miller and the salty seaside postcards of Donald McGill – a world where a man with his trousers around his ankles in an optician's would be told by his lady examiner, "No, no, Mr Smith! I said, 'Could I see your worn *spectacles*?'"

It was Max, the cheeky chappie, who found his passage up a narrow hill road blocked by a pretty girl. (What happened? Obvious, isn't it? He tossed himself off.)

As I write, Mollie Sudgen has just passed away and Twitter is ablaze with her character Mrs Slocombe's unforgettable gaffes about her cat, taken from her role in *Are You Being Served?* – including such peaches as, "If my pussy isn't attended to by eight o'clock, I shall be stroking it for the rest of the evening!"

At the first sign of a danger the hair on Mrs Slocombe's pussy stood on end. It gasped all night during a heatwave and once, when the central heating broke down, she confided, "I had to light the oven and hold my pussy in front of it."

Childish, maybe. Puerile, certainly. But *very* funny.

The humble *double entendre* has endured via the comedy of Dick Emery, *Viz* comic and Barry Humphries, whose coarse creation Sir Les Patterson was enjoying a warm hand on his entrance long before Julian Clary ever did. This modest collection stands proudly in that vulgar but vital tradition. I believe that the best of these howlers deserve to be remembered just as much as the scripted one-liners of the *Carry On* films. (See my *Carry On* tribute on page 101).

Garry's Goofs are a constant reminder that we all make verbal howlers – even me. Why, only last month I was asked about the goofs on a radio show and stated, quite reasonably I felt, "I have an innuendo detector and believe me it's a large one."

I also once told an interviewer that I wasn't interested in getting involved in politics with a big 'P'... now why did that make the studio engineer start giggling?

Garry Bushell

Twenty Of The Best

While talking about snowfall, back when she was a humble TVAM weathergirl, Ulrika Jonsson delivered the all-time classic goof: "I had a good eight inches last night!"

Racing driver Jenson Button was discussing driving in high winds, when he revealed, "It was like my helmet was being sucked off!"

Here's weightlifting commentator Pat Glenn, talking about a particularly impressive contender, Tatiana *Gregoriava*: "This is Gregoriava from Bulgaria. I saw her snatch this morning and it was amazing."

Jack Barnicle, talking about Colin Edwards's motorbike tyres on *World Superbikes*, commented: "Colin had a hard on in practice earlier, and I bet he wished he had a hard on now."

This startling pronouncement was made by Brian Moore, when he was commentating on Dutch footballer Johan de Kock at Euro 96: "De Kock has come up for this one; this could cause a massive problem . . ."

When Philippa Forrester cuddled a male astronomer for warmth during BBC1's eclipse coverage, Michael Buerk goofed: "They seem cold out there, they're rubbing each other and he has come in his shorts."

This beauty comes from Ken Brown, talking about golfing legend Nick Faldo and his caddy Fanny Sunneson who were lining up shots at the Scottish Open: "Some weeks Nick likes to use Fanny, other weeks he prefers to do it by himself."

Bobby Simpson, discussing a fine piece of bowling from cricketer Neil Fairbrother on Sky Sports, observed: "With his lovely soft hands he just tossed it off."

Matt Baker was talking about the proud city of Liverpool, when he announced on *Blue Peter*, "No visit to the docks would be complete without a tug." Not the first time I've heard that said…

Richard Whiteley(RIP) asked Carol Barnes if she could beat the contestants' six-letter words on Channel 4's *Countdown*. "Yes," she said proudly, "I got aroused."

Racing Post's Stewart Machin, commentating on jockey Tony McCoy's formidable lead: "Tony has a quick look between his legs and likes what he sees."

Andrea McLean, starting a men's bike race on GMTV, told the male competitors: "When I give you the horn, you have to go for it."

John Virgo, discussing Ronnie O'Sullivan's snooker playing technique: "Sometimes he follows through with such force he knocks the chalk out of his pockets."

Kate Charman on *Guinness World Records*, as five bikers were about to roar round a wall of death with a woman standing in the middle: "Robin is completely exposed; their helmets are just inches from her head."

Carol Baxter trying to identify an apple by biting into it on TV-am, said: "This one tastes like Cox."

Maureen Madill reporting from the Women's Open golf: "Sherri Steinhauser has a good healthy crack, and Ken Brown will take a closer look at it." Lucky Ken.

Lorna Clark, talking about riding techniques at the Badminton Horse Trials: "Andrew Hoy is such a perfectionist he'll give his horse head to get him over a fence." Blimey, most horses will settle for a bag of oats . . .

Mike Hallett made this shocking announcement when talking about missed shots on Sky's Premier League Snooker: "Steven Hendry jumps on Steve Davis's misses every chance he gets."

Andy Jameson at the Commonwealth Games, talking about Aussie swimming star Michael Klim's height: "Klim is a big guy, a very big guy. When he's got his kit off, the length is frightening."

Former West Ham soccer hero Tony Gale gave Sky Sports football fans a shocking insight into Cristiano Ronaldo when he commented: "Ronaldo goes down too easily for my liking but remember he's literally got two big men up his backside for 90 minutes."

The Classics

Desmond Morris opened the door of the gents' toilet at a zoo on *Animal Roadshow*, to show Sarah Kennedy the beautiful birds inside. "There's been a cockatoo in there," he told her. She seemed quite taken aback.

Margaret Thatcher was talking about her Home Secretary, Willie Whitelaw, when she revealed, "Every Prime Minister needs a Willie." Well, she already had more balls than most blokes . . .

Commentating on the Oxford-Cambridge Boat Race, Harry Carpenter raised many an eyebrow when he observed, "Ah, isn't that nice? The wife of the Cambridge president is kissing the cox of the Oxford crew."

Arthur Negus was most impressed by two glass decanters on *Antiques Roadshow*, telling their busty female owner, "That's the nicest pair I've seen in ages."

Ian Botham failed to step over his wicket while playing the West Indies at cricket. As Jonathan Agnew remarked, "He didn't quite manage to get his leg over." Unusual for Beefy, that . . .

Craig Charles was talking about the rules of the contest on

cult TV game show *Takeshi's Castle*, when he announced, "If your ring is penetrated you're out of the game." Obviously these rules don't apply if you work at the Beeb . . .

Racing commentator Julian Wilson was discussing Goodwood jockeys when he remarked to trainer Josh Gifford, "I suppose the best ride around the place is your daughter?"

Chain Letters presenter Allan Stewart was discussing a six foot five contestant called Richard when he told two women competitors, "That's enough Dick for both of you!"

And here's cricket commentator Brian Johnston on classic form, talking about Michael Holding and Peter Willey during a Test Match: "The bowler's Holding, the batsman's Willey."

Foot in Mouth Disease – Sports Clangers

Being a live sports commentator is one of the hardest jobs in broadcasting; requiring the ability to sum up the excitement of an event along with an encyclopaedic knowledge of names and past glories...not that this should ever stop us from enjoying their mistakes.

David Coleman: "That's the fastest time ever run, but it's not as fast as the world record."

Brough Scott: "And there's the unmistakable figure of Joe Mercer . . . or is it Lester Piggott?"

Clive Allen: "We've seen this sort of déjà vu before."

Dan Maskell: "And here come the Gullikson twins, both from Wisconsin."

Rio Ferdinand: "Gary Neville was captain, and now Ryan Giggs has taken on the mantelpiece."

Dion Dublin: "When United create chances they always take them; Ronaldo had one there and didn't take it."

ITV's Clive Tyldesley, talking about Bayern Munich: "Next season Bayern will be playing in a brand new spanking stadium." Sounds like the sort of place Max Mosley would enjoy . . .

Virgina Wade: "Winning matches is the best recipe for winning."

Ricky Hatton: "I've gone from being a global champion to being a worldwide champion."

Twenty More of my All-Time Favourite Goofs

Chris Tarrant was trying to help a female contestant name a famous motor-racing commentator; the answer was Murray Walker: "I'll give you a clue," said Chris, "his name sounds like something hard that tastes good when you suck it." "Ah," she replied, "it must be Dickie Davies."

Annabel Croft was talking about the coming Wimbledon tennis semi-finals on GMTV when she said: "This time next week Tim Henman will hope that he's at least got a semi on."

Shock news from the BBC's Crufts coverage, when Peter Purves revealed: "Michael Parkinson has entered a stylish black bitch." It was never like that on Blue Peter.

South African medic Dr Mensalalei, discussing circumcision: "Women are insisting boys be given medical examinations before they go into the bush." These days, it's probably for the best.

Paul Dickenson got worked while commentating on the 'Dead Weight Lift' round on *Britain's Strongest Man*, excitedly saying: "Glenn Ross, 200 kilograms swinging between his legs, hoping to get it up . . ." Now that'd be something to see . . .

Here's an eyewitness talking about gas spillage from the BBC's News South West: "One minute he was unloading gas and the next thing we knew his ring had split and we had to be evacuated." Nasty . . .

Telly chef Delia Smith, gave this advice about preparing a crispy duck on her How To Cook series: "You need extra pricks down there where the thigh meets the body."

An unexpected insight from Clare Balding at the Grand National: "If the horse takes off too soon, it can ejaculate the jockey."

David Goldstrum, commentating on the European Weightlifting championship: "Ruth Kasyrie's body weight means she's lost a bronze medal in the snatch. But she can get it back with a good clean and jerk."

Bill Oddie, talking about birds on BBC2's *Springwatch* and *not* about the fragrant Kate Humble: "The great tits have gone, her box is empty . . . there's a chance of shags on Shetland next week."

Chris Brady, talking about how he'd present his meal to fellow contestant Shaida Shipping on Channel 4's entertaining dinner party show, *Come Dine with Me*: "I can't wait to get her round my place, pin her to the floor and stick it down her throat." Steady on, mate!

Gay ex-cop Brian Paddick, getting worked up about Timmy Mallett's alleged cheating tactics on ITV's *I'm a Celebrity . . . Get Me Out of Here*: "He dug his nails into my arm to stop me swallowing."

Judy Finnigan, asking viewers about Richard Madeley's beard

INNUENDO BONANZA!

on ITV's *This Morning*: "Let me know if I should make Richard have it off by lunchtime."

Alistair Appleton, while trying to find a city couple a rural house on BBC2's *Escape to the Country*, confided: "Both work from home so they're always on top of each other."

Hugh Fearnley-Whittingstall was actually talking about a fishing net when he told viewers of his Channel 4 show *River Cottage*: "I'm having some trouble getting my end away."

Here's the ever reliable Ulrika Jonsson chatting to Eddie Irvine about Miss World contenders: "Eddie, you must have come across some of the most beautiful girls in the world."

Gino D'Acampo, boasting about his food to Carol Thatcher on ITV's *Christmas Cooks Challenge*: "Once I put it in your mouth, you will never want anything else."

Here's a delighted customer describing a designer motorbike to Paul Teutal on the Discovery Channel's *American Chopper*: "I'm just so happy to sit on such a beautiful chopper."

Michael Baggett, raving about a watch that a woman brought in for valuation on *Flog It!*, drooled: "My eyes nearly popped out of my head when I saw you open your lovely little box in the queue."

Gay designer Scott Hensall, discussing his Yorkshire puddings (probably) on ITV's *Britain's Best Celebrity Dish*: "I've never done small ones, I've only ever done big."

Foot in Mouth Disease – Sports Clangers II

Murray Walker: "There is Michael Schumacher. He's in a very good position. He's in last place."

Mark Bright: "It's win or bust for them, although a draw will do."

Jeremy Guscott on drug tests: "Brian Moore got tested after every single game in the World Cup and it really got up his nose."

Kate Silverton: "You were up against the Norwegians who were quite literally born on skis."

Manish Bhasin: "Are Paraguay expecting England to play ugly with Peter Crouch upfront?"

Brian Johnston: "You've come over at a very appropriate time; Ray Illingworth has just relieved himself at the pavilion end."

Frank McLintock on the FA Cup: "I'm predicting a Millwall victory but I think Sunderland will win."

David Begg: "And the Celtic supporters, holding their heads in their faces . . ."

Dion Dublin: "No player has scored 40 goals in a season . . . although Clive Allen did."

Lawrence Dallaglio: "Obviously the changing room's full of ecstasy and everybody's happy." *A-c-ii-ddd!*

Huw Edwards: "Very unusually it has turned noon here in Washington."

Morning Glory

They get up at silly o'clock to bring us news, reviews and gossip over our breakfast. So it's hardly surprising that early morning TV presenters are responsible for more big clangers than a bell-making factory...

Ever wondered what *GMTV* presenters do when the cameras are off? Here's Fiona Phillips to explain: "We've worked out what we can do in the break. Just lie back on the sofa and spread your legs . . ."

Here's a classic howler from Lorraine Kelly on *GMTV*: "This year's hairstyle is called the Shag and our resident stylist is here to give our model one."

Kate Garraway, talking about twin baby girls on *GMTV*: "I can't believe anything so pink and soft can make a woman so desperate."

Penny Smith, talking about Richard Arnold kissing Kate Garraway, after some couples renewed their wedding vows live on *GMTV*: "We had to pull him off an organ and now we'll have to pull him off Kate." The 'organ' I can believe...

And not to be out-done, here's cuddly Eamonn Holmes, rabbiting away about a blood pressure monitor: "Me and Fiona haven't had it off since Christmas," he said.

Susan Brookes, talking about encountering a bull on *This Morning*: "I never thought I'd ever find myself stroking something so big."

Bill Turnbull, discussing Aleem Maqbool's Christmas trek from Nazareth to Jerusalem on *BBC Breakfast*: "You've worn out four donkeys and I can't see us getting another donkey to go with you."

Fiona Phillips, startling studio guest Kevin Williams when discussing the Pussycat Dolls on *GMTV*: "We'll see if we can get a photo of you and the pussies later."

Here's gaffe-prone Fiona talking about media stars on *GMTV*: "The big ones are always the nicest."

And here she is again, talking about a lion being released into the wild: "That's the first smell of an African bush he's had in 12 years."

Of course not all of the howlers Fiona was involved with were filthy. Who could forget the time she interviewed a man whose unfortunate wife had been mauled by feral dogs? "So," she said. "Do the police know who owns the dogs?" "No," the husband replied. "But they're working on a couple of leads."

Kate Garraway, talking about mispronounced place names on *GMTV* and assuring a delighted Ben Shepherd: "Whatever you give me now, I'll get my lips around it."

Pop news: according to *GMTV*, "Elton John blew 40 million in 20 months." He can't be expected to name them all, of course . . .

Pause for Sport

Here's Harry Carpenter proving that anything can happen in sport. The veteran voice of boxing was commentating on the Muhammad Ali-George Foreman fight. These are his exact words: "Suddenly Ali looks very tired indeed; in fact Ali at times now looks as though he can barely lift his arms up . . . Oh he's got him with a right hand! He's got him! Oh you can't believe it. And I don't think Foreman's going to get up. He's trying to beat the count. And he's out! OH MY GOD he's won the title back at 32! Muhammad Ali!"

Dennis Taylor, talking to Willie Thorne about Jimmy White's snooker game with Matthew Stevens: "I really fancy Jimmy's green Willie, and if he hits Matthew in the back with it . . ." it'll be quite a trick shot!

Stuart Storey, commentating on the 100-metre hurdles: "Britain's Sarah Claxton has got a small Pole inside her and she'll come with an explosion." Blimey!

Jonathan Edwards, clearly blown away by long-jumper Phillips Idowu's performance at the 2007 World Indoor Athletics: "An absolutely massive one – and he's proved himself after pulling it off in the first round of the national trials."

Mick Tucker reporting from the Burghley Horse Trial: "Lucinda Fredericks, a reluctant ride, but as Captain Mark Philips told her, 'It's very small Lucinda, but it's good enough to do the big one.'"

Sir Clive Woodward, talking about the British Lions: "In that changing room I'm smelling a group of men all coming together."

Mark Durden-Smith, covering the 1997 Boat Race for ITV: "The Cambridge crew now have to toss their cox into the water. Is this enjoyable, James Cracknell?"

Peter Allis, discussing a Rosie Jones shot at the Weetabix Ladies Golf Open: "She'll need a good whack to get it up."

A Leeds United fan, remembering Billy Bremner: "We'd clean the dressing room, then Billy would come in, the balls would come out and we'd have a game of two-touch."

Gary Herbert, reporting from the 2004 World Cup: "One of sport's great sights – men powering away, Matthew Pinsent exploding into his guys and Alex Partridge happy to have his length."

The Antiques Goof Show

TV antique shows have been delighting viewers for decades. Along with precious relics, old masters and collectibles the programmes have long been appreciated for their treasure trove of howlers....

Art expert Clive Stewart-Lockhart, talking about a painting on *Antiques Roadshow*: "It's a fine portrait of an angelic-looking lovely young lady . . . the only problem is she has definitely been touched up."

Auctioneer Paul Laidlaw, describing an antique walking came on *Bargain Hunt*: "It's a good length, ladies and gentlemen . . . they're frequently too short."

Paul Martin had a degree of doubt crossing his mind as he admired a painting of a cat on *Flog It! Ten of the Best*: "Will there be interest at the auction for our pussy portrait?"

Here's a verbatim conversation about a fairground Wurlitzer from *The Great Antiques Hunt*. Jilly Goolden: "I don't suppose everybody could fit it in." Male expert: "No, it's a very large organ."

Paul Laidlaw, enthusing about a silver carafe on *Bargain Hunt*: "If you pull it out after a dinner party, your guests are going to go, 'Wow!'"

David Batty, getting quite carried away while examining a bowl with a pineapple lid on *Antiques Road Show*: "This is the most magical, wonderful knob I have ever seen."

Martin Roberts, on a lady's newly purchased house in *Under the Hammer*: "Everything looked okay until we saw the crack she had in the living room."

James Lewis, talking about jugs with Tim Wonnacott on *Bargain Hunt*: "Whenever you see jugs, you like to see a pair of jugs." I know I do!

Angela Rippon, describing the public response to a female contestant's antiques on *Sun, Sea and Bargain Spotting*: "It's been a few hours and there's still no interest in her chest whatsoever."

Mark Stacey, describing an orange glass vase on *Bargain Hunt*: "Whenever I handle it, it looks just like a big sweet and I want to lick it."

In Praise of Ainsley Harriott

Let's take a moment to celebrate a telly presenter who enjoys a good cock-up almost as much as I do. Ainsley Harriott speaks such fluent innuendo that *The Sun* once dubbed him "the TV chef who talks in pure Garry's Goofs". Here are just a few howlers from his long history of serial goofing, all of them delivered on either *Can't Cook Won't Cook* or *Ready Steady Cook*:

Talking about beef, Ainsley told viewers: "Get your hands in there and give your meat a good rub."

About a kitchen tool: "He handles his chopper well, doesn't he?"

About cooking onions for breakfast: "I like a good toss in the morning, don't you?"

And naturally, Ainsley was discussing a kebab skewer when he assured us, "If it's moist it goes in easier."

I'd printed several of Harriott's food-related howlers before I began to suspect that the flamboyant North London-born star was doing it on purpose. Was Ainsley cheating? I immediately fixed up a meeting with the TV cook famous for his big floppy (hat, that is). He was unashamedly proud of his mentions in my columns.

"I've been in Garry's Goofs at least five times in the last year," he beamed. "The last time I was talking about a long-handled spoon and I said, 'You need something with a nice length on it so you can pop it inside.'

"What's wrong with that, Gal?" he asked, as innocent as a cat with cream-speckled whiskers. "It's just your mind."

Yeah, right. Come on, I persisted, Paxman-like, these are pre-scripted aren't they?

Ainsley smiled like the Sphinx but would give nothing away. "I always try to make food sexy," he said finally. "It helps viewers relate to it. The traditional approach to cooking is too serious. They tell you to take one egg and two ounces of whatever, it's boring. But when you say, 'Take your egg and slide it into your hole . . . there, isn't that lovely?' then that oozes fun.

"It sounds saucy. But I'm not actually telling women to drag their husbands off to the woods and ravish them. Although if they've got time . . ."

And that was it. But, deliberate or not, the Harriott approach worked a treat. Viewers loved him and he lit up our screens like a huge shaft . . . of sunshine.

Years later, Nigella Lawson followed his lead, suggestively handling her vegetables and unleashing her own non-stop barrage of double entendres. In Nigella's kitchen everything was soft, moist, luscious and warm. "These are my guilty secrets," she'd say. "They really are bulging."

But did she mean her mincemeat pies or the ample contents of her clinging scarlet sweater?

Newspaper sub-editors gleefully joined in the fun writing headlines like 'Nigella likes a good stuffing' and 'Nigella likes men with balls'.

Goofs Galore

Keith Chegwin, when knocking up Lord Bath on Channel 4's much-missed *The Big Breakfast*, told startled viewers: "Fingers crossed we can look around his private parts." He wouldn't be the first . . .

Was Mike Tucker boasting or discussing show-jumping when he said, "Helen Lundback in a key position, riding Madick"? Madick was a horse, of course.

On *Police Action Live*, reporter Anya Seetherum told WPC Doreen Davos: "I spent a night with you in the back of this car, and it was pretty hairy."

As contestant Heather faced a risky ice challenge on channel Five's *Unbreakable*, the voiceover man informed us: "Leaving her concerns with her underwear, she's the first to brave the hole." Crikey!

Long distance runner Paula Radcliffe talking about a race on BBC1's sports comedy show *They Think It's All Over*, revealed: "I've only been lapped once and that was indoors." It leaves a funny taste in the mouth, apparently.

James May was enthusing about one-man flying machines on his Big Ideas series when he told amazed BBC2 viewers: "I'm here to try another smaller strap-on chopper."

Jodie Kidd, talking about the men's makeup routine on *Strictly Come Dancing: It Takes Two*: "The boys are in there all the time being touched up." Tsk. I don't know, that Bruno Tonioli . . .

Here's Clive Anderson discussing body posture with ballet dancer Darcy Bussell on his ITV show: "I'm holding myself erect just talking to you."

Louis Walsh, chatting to Holly Willoughby on ITV2's *Xtra Factor*, asked if she'd come again; Heavenly Holly replied: "I wouldn't come on my own but I'd come in a crowd." I'd pay to see that . . .

Hulk Hogan was referring to the swimming pool when he asked the gorgeous Venom, on *American Gladiator*, "How about getting Monica wet this time?" She assured him she was "excited and ready for more".

Gay Richard, wittering away about their performance on BBC2's *The Restaurant*, told boyfriend Scott: "We've been in the bottom ever since we met Raymond."

Bill Threlfall, talking about tennis ace Mark Petchey's style on Sky Sports: "He's just got married and that should harden him up."

Christopher St John Smith, talking about the beach volleyball on Eurosport, told us: "The Brazilian girls on top of the Norwegian sisters . . . who gets the deep poke?" The luckiest one, I guess . . .

A female contestant, demonstrating how to make sausages on *The Generation Game* back in the 90s assured Bruce Forsyth:

"You can't beat doing it by hand."

Lowri Turner, talking about high heels on *Looking Good*: "Some women will do anything for that extra three inches."

Coach Trip director Brendan was on about a Swiss mountain, not a flat-chested female contestant, when he told male travellers: "Today you're all going to Mount Titlis."

Tom Hughes, commentating on Eurosports's tree-felling show *Timbersports*, made the potentially libellous accusation: "Two men going at it in Obersdorf, and both of them take the chopper round the other side." Dirty sods . . .

Genuine quote from the 2009 Chelsea Flower Show brochure: "Nothing says summer more than a sweet pea in the garden."

Contestant Angie chatting about rival Barry's soup on *Come Dine with Me*: "I wasn't too sure about the thickness but he assured me that it was just right." Well, he would, wouldn't he?

Robin Cousins, discussing Gemma and Andre's skating on *Dancing on Ice*: "You should have some nice positions, it's a bit stiff but that helps him. Just relax through it."

Pause for Sport II

On *The World's Strongest Man*, Nick Halling revealed Stefan Petursson was "in the lead with four fingers in an impressive 28 seconds". Although I suspect he could beat that if he dated Shirley Carter on *EastEnders* . . .

Formula 1 driver Felipe Massa reckons his lucky white underpants help him win races: "These pants have ten victories and 14 pole positions."

Colin Bryce, commentating on the Men's Luge: "Edney on top, Pfister slides into his bottom section and this is an exciting ride."

Stuart Storey makes an astonishing claim about tri-athlete Jodie Swallow: "There are plenty of girls who can take it out early and give you a nice stroke and Swallow's in amongst it."

Gymnastics commentator Mitch Fenner, talking about Anton *Golotsutskov*: "He needs to get the legs open and shove his head in, but he's come almost as soon as he's left the horse."

John Virgo, commenting on a Ronnie O'Sullivan snooker shot: "That was brilliant, especially as he only has two or three inches to play with."

David Pleat, commentating on the Chelsea v Cluj game: "Kone's pulled off Alex at the back post."

Tracy Austin, reporting from Wimbledon: "Castano probing deep but she's lost her vibration dampener and even Martina Navratalova can't find it." And if Martina can't find it . . .

Stuart Storey, discussing runner Wilson Kipketer's tactics for the 800metres: "He can do it any way, he can take them from the front or he can take them from the rear."

Les Ferdinand, talking about Fulham v Man United on *Final Score*: "The goalkeeper slipped on his back and somebody went down on him."

Mark Petchey, reporting from Wimbledon: "Andy Murray goes in for a bit of self-abuse, whacking himself so hard his knuckles start to bleed."

Goofs, Gaffes and Glamour Girls

Not all good-looking TV glamour girls are air-heads, but we give regular thanks for the ones that are...and to the following beauties who, despite having brains as big as their breasts, accidentally ended up with egg on their faces...

A miu miu is a kind of dog, but *Sunday Sport* favourite Zoe Anderson must still have turned on some onanistic *Men and Motors* viewers when she confided: "I just lay there stroking my miu miu until she got excited."

The late Natalie Turner was talking about conkers when she advised viewers: "They need to soak their nuts in vinegar; it's the only way they'll ever be hard enough."

Glam goddess Vikki Thomas, talking about a 1970s style space-hopper: "I love having something large and bouncy between my legs."

Paris Hilton talking about a US supermarket chain: "Wal-Marts, do they like make walls there?" D'oh!

Here's Granada *Men and Motors*' TV beauty Zoe Anderson again, commenting on a team of bikers wearing the same colour headwear: "Ooh, look at their lovely purple helmets, that's quite a display."

And here's Vikki Thomas talking about a winter cold virus: "I managed to avoid it all over Christmas but I'm definitely getting it now. I spent all yesterday on my back in bed with the curtains shut."

Glamour goddess Jo Guest was discussing drinking pints of beer on *British Tribes* when she goofed: "It's quite nice to have something big in your hand." And a good head is not to be sniffed at either.

Kerry Katona: "I spend a lot of my life in the back of cars – woops, I didn't mean that the way it sounded. Like, hence the two kids…"

Page Three legend Sam Fox demonstrating her brains: "I've got ten pairs of trainers, one for every day of the week."

Here's Natalie Turner again, talking about a bad game of golf on my own series Garry Bushell Reveals All: "My boyfriend took about 30 strokes before he finally managed to shoot onto the green."

Foot in Mouth – Sports Clangers III

Murray Walker: "The car in front is absolutely unique, except for the one behind which is identical."

Chris Kamara: "The Emirates stadium cost hardly any money, £250million I think."

Alan Curbishley: "There were four players I wanted to look at: Carroll, McCartney, Tevez, Noble and Carlton Cole."

David Pleat: "Ronaldo has been compared to George Best, the incomparable George Best."

Paul Jewell on Wigan: "I wasn't particularly enamelled with the way we played."

Chris Kamara: "QPR had eight attempts on goal. They missed the target four times, worked the keeper on four occasions, and hit the bar twice."

Les Ferdinand: "There's no expectation anymore with Northern Ireland. They expect to win games."

David Bentley: "I hope I'm not a 21-year-old player forever."

Netball commentator Jo Binns: "Romelda Aitken is unstoppable. The way to stop her is to stop the ball getting in to her hands."

Arun Lal on Zaheer Khan: "He is literally making the ball talk."

Paul Masefield: "Ronaldo can pull anything out of the hat at the drop of a whim."

Terry Venables: "When you think about players like Larsson and Ljungberg, those are the players you think about."

Pause for Sport III

Noel Thompson, talking about golf on *BBC Breakfast* to a startled Sonia Deol: "It doesn't matter how long it takes, when it finally goes in the hole it's a very special feeling." I'll say . . .

Peter Alliss, discussing a Lee Westwood golf shot at the Open: "Westwood has left himself a little tickler for a 69." Nice . . .

John Virgo, talking about snooker technique: "Neil Robertson's main concern is getting a deep screw with plenty of bottom."

David Vine, raving about a female weightlifter at the Olympics: "This lady is magnificent; she already has a 158kg snatch under her belt."

John Barrett, gleefully enthusing about Wimbledon ladies' tennis action: "Sharapova, fist pumping away, she's hitting a lot of meaty balls."

Andy Townsend, talking about Jan Koller during the Turkey v Czech Republic match: "During the first 15 minutes, Cervet was literally, literally, right up his backside."

Alan Green, discussing Kenwyne Jones' injury during the

Trinidad & Tobago v England match: "Any knock to that wrist and he'd come right off."

David Goldstrum, talking about the women's weightlifting on Eurosport: "Marzena Karpinska cleans, jerks well and is very comfortable in the snatch."

Neil Adams, reporting from the World Judo Cup: "Sophie Johnstone, head between the Spanish girl's legs . . . but will she be able to find her Waza-ari?"

Race ace Derek Thompson, talking about the wind at Cheltenham: "You stand here and suddenly you're blown off." Result!

Ian Botham made this surprise revelation while discussing pre-match rituals on Sky Sport 2: "I always liked a quick rub to get rid of stiffness."

Goofs Galore II

Bjork was trying to have a serious conversation about singles when she confided to Jo Whiley: "It's hard to get seven inches in Iceland." Must be the cold weather . . .

Contestant Julia, describing Danny's starter course on *Come Dine with Me*: "I loved it in my mouth and couldn't wait to have some more."

Zoe Martlew, talking about Alex James conducting on *Maestro*: "We're seeing a lot of what Alex wants from his right hand."

Christine Still, exclaiming on Russian Anna Pavlova's amazing gymnastic performance at the Summer Olympics: "Lovely tight legs, she lifts before she twists and comes off at exactly the right moment." That takes real skill . . .

A chap called Michael, speculating about how fellow contestant Bruce would perform on *Come Dine with Me* opined: "I think he's going to pull it off tonight."

Ken Livingstone, talking about Uri Geller's spoon trick to Jason Manford on Channel 4, said: "He puts it on your hand and it just goes limp."

The ever-cheeky Colin Bryce, reporting on a weightlifting event on World's Strongest Man, told us: "Bulgaria's strongest man, posterior pumping . . . it means more pain for Boyer." Sounds like Boyer better mind his back . . .

Here's sour-faced 'dragon' Deborah Meaden talking about musical instruments at BBC2's *First Night at the Proms*: "I would find it hard to handle a new organ for every performance."

Alan Parry, talking about contestant Katie's performance on *Gladiators: Hang Tough*, revealed: "She hung for dear life as Tempest tried to pull her and her pants off."

Jules Hudson amused fans of cockney rhyming slang, by asking a couple who wanted a property with a paddock on *Escape to the Country*: "How do you feel about having a little pony in there?" (For non-Londoners, that's pony and trap = crap).

Gobby Gregg Wallace urged Andy Peters on BBC1's *Celebrity Masterchef* to: "Make a bald man very happy with your banana muffin."

Josie D'Arby relived a classic goof when, amazed by the sight of a pink parakeet on Channel 4's *The Bigger Breakfast*: "I've seen a cockatoo in my time. But none as big as this."

Shopping Channel Shockers

TV Shopping Channel presenters are tasked with chatting endlessly and feigning excitement about some of the most mundane household goods available for purchase; is it any wonder then that double meanings occasionally get the better of them?

Dishy Debbie Flint, waxing lyrical about a telescope on One TV (Channel 670) to a male expert: "It's very big. How long does it take you to get it fully erect then?" (For you, Deb? Nanoseconds.)

Here's Debbie again, bigging up a bracelet on One TV: "Seven inches should fit anybody."

Debbie Greenwood was brushing hair from a bloke's trousers with a house broom on QVC, when she looked at the front of his strides and exclaimed: "What an amazing tool!"

Adele Sica, flogging a set of towels on Price-Drop TV: "Noticed my ring, did you? I'll be selling that within the hour." I'll start the bidding at a fiver!

Elisa Portelli raised eyebrows by talking about a space-hopper on Bid-Up TV: "You sit on those big balls and grip the ears," she said.

QVC's Paul Lavers was actually talking about dishing up a meal when he enthused: "I would like to plate you and have you mounted." Still a big shock for the female chef though . . .

Sean Macintosh, auctioning a diamond ring on Bid TV: "Imagine the evening, ladies. He gets it out, puts it on the table and slides it across . . ."

Here's Adam Hepperston demonstrating a cordless drill on Bid TV: "I'm really in the mood to do a bit of screwing now."

David Ades, demonstrating a carpet cleaner with Debbie Flint on Price Crash TV: "Obviously, when you buy the kit, you're not going to be on your hands and knees with a scrubber."

Joanne Patrick got an unexpected surprise on *Ideal World* when a male colleague who was making coffee with a Bamix Hand Blender turned to her and said: "Would you just hold it for me for a moment Joanne, just until it rises."

Of course, the biggest shopping channel cock-up occurred this summer, when two 'live' channels were apparently fronted by the same host – at the same time. In August 2009, *The Sun* revealed that Paul Evers had presented seemingly real-time auctions on both Bid TV and Price-Drop TV one Friday lunchtime – wearing exactly the same orange shirt.

The two channels both had the word 'Live' in the top right-hand corner of the screener. Just after 2pm, crop-haired Paul was encouraging viewers on Bid TV to ring in for goods including mobiles and iPod speakers. Simultaneously, he was urging people to snap up home phone systems on Price-Drop TV.

One puzzled viewer asked *The Sun*, "If the channel isn't live, how can the host claim to know how many are being sold?" Boss Ian Percival told the paper that the actual bidding on both channels was live, but he admitted host Paul's spiel on Price-Drop TV was recorded. It was a cost-cutting move, he explained . . .

Goofs Galore III

Mark Evans, talking about a plant on BBC1's *Garden Invaders* to a startled female contestant: "Your next prize is nestled between my legs."

Carol McGiffin was discussing beds, mercifully, on ITV's *Loose Women* when she revealed: "I tried a soft one but I hated it. I like hard ones."

Prue Leith, talking about flavour on BBC2's *The Great British Menu*, confided: "If it doesn't come off in the mouth it's just a joke." Indeed . . .

Casualty star Georgia Taylor was describing a below ankle amputation on Channel 4's *The Paul O'Grady Show*, when Paul told her: "I've got a foot under the desk that I've got to show you." Steady on!

A lad described a scantily-clad girl being carried into her party on MTV's *My Super Sweet Sixteen*: "No one has ever seen an entrance like hers before," he said.

Gordon Ramsay was discussing meatballs on *The F-Word*, when he asked former Spice Girl Geri Halliwell: "How many balls at any one time have you had in your mouth?" What a thing to ask the woman, I mean, it's not as if she's one of his girlfriends...

Top chef Delia Smith, talking about her curry evenings with friends on *Delia*, said: "Everybody's having a bit of everybody else's and I think that's really good." The posh ones are the worst.

House-hunter Marion talking about gardens on *Location, Location, Location* to Channel 4's Kirstie Allsopp: "I'd much rather have length than width." Each to her own.

Muscleman Leonard, 72, talking about weight training on ITV's *Britain's Got Talent* told Amanda Holden: "At my age you've really got to work to keep it up."

A Scottish holidaymaker enthusing about a local hotel and *not* the resort's thriving gay scene told The One Show's reporter: "I come back to Blackpool every year because I really love the Queen's."

Quizmania's Greggles Scott was like a magnet for idiots. This exchange with a live caller isn't a classic goof, but it is very funny. Asked to give the name of an occupation beginning with a 'T' a Scouse lady rang up and said "A doctor." Greggles groaned "Is Sesame Street on any more?" adding "We need an occupation beginning with 'T'." "Oh," she replied. "A dentist."

Pause for Sport IV

John Barrett was commentating on tennis play at the Australian Open when he described Marat Safin as: "The big man whose wrist is working the balls well and scattering seeds all over the tournament."

Clare Balding, discussing horse trainer Deidre Johnston: "Deidre's a lovely girl and she manages to keep all the owners satisfied." No wonder she looks knackered . . .

Vincent Walduck talked himself into the Goof Hall of Fame with his vivid commentary on synchronised trampolining: "These two American girls can bounce seven metres above the bed, come together, give it a full twist, half in and half out, and then dismount with a ball out."

Sterling Sharpe was describing the action at the US Superbowl when he said: "Helmet to helmet contact. Randy Gay is banged up by the Giants."

Matt Le Tissier, talking about the Blackburn v Everton game on Sky Sports: "McCarthy was just about to shoot when he was taken from behind." That's enough to put anyone off . . .

Dennis Taylor, commenting on a snooker shot at the Masters to Willie Thorne: "He's got a choice. He can either take the brown or the pink, Willie."

Attractive pole-vault champion Kate Dennison raised eyebrows when she proudly revealed: "I'm in the right physical shape to get on the longer poles."

Karen Brown, talking rather dismissively about the men's hockey at the Olympics: "It's no good being good and hard if you can't hit the target."

Lydia Hislop, handing over to Mike Cattermole for the 1.20 race on Racing UK: "We'll soon have them off, here comes Mike with the big one."

Andy Gray commentating on Liverpool v Luton for Sky Sports One: "Benayoun has been stuck inside Dirk Kuyt for most of the second half." That takes stamina . . .

Nick Halling, talking about the Atlas balls on *The World's Strongest Man*: "He takes a grip but, the sweatier these men get, the harder it is to get any purchase on their balls; especially when they weigh 160 kilos."

Rugby commentator Andrew Cotter, soberly analysing a Scottish player's mistake: "Look at the replay and you'll see Sean Lamont totally exposes himself."

David Goldstrum. talking about impressive female weightlifter Jang Mi-ran: "She's more than 18 stone and that's disregarding that snatch."

And The Goofs Go On

Cliff Richard opened up about wanting to be Elvis Presley when he was younger on BBC4's *Pop Britannica*: "I'd have liked to have woken up and found I was inside him," he revealed.

There was an Irish theme on ITV's *Loose Women* when Jackie Brambles introduced Lynda Bellingham: "There isn't anyone who doesn't like her craic." I hope it's less lumpy than her gravy . . .

Kate Humble, talking about catching a wild rhino with a helicopter on BBC2's Animal Park: "It can get a bit dangerous if he gets his chopper to the bush."

Letitia Dean didn't win *Strictly Come Dancing*, but she certainly gets a goofing gold for telling that old fool Brucie: "Every time I feel my head is far enough back, I want another 12 inches." Good game, good game!

Hugh Fearnley-Whittingstall, talking about a sumptuous medieval banquet on *River Cottage Xmas Feast*, told us: "Hopefully, I'll impress the guests with my magnificent, meaty centrepiece." He also mentioned a "ten-bird roast" – a big favourite with Premiership footballers, apparently.

Virginia Wade, discussing an impressive tennis shot during

BBC1's Wimbledon tennis coverage: "Justine Henin-Hardenne – come onto her stomach and I'll guarantee she'll whip it."

Anna Ryder Richardson was chatting about her instructor's diving gear on *I'm a Celebrity...Get Me Out Of Here* when she revealed: "Rodney is quite huge and the helmet was massive and really heavy."

Jonty Hearnden was attempting to find the maker's name on an old violin, on *Cash in the Attic*, when he told the surprised female owner: "I've just had a sneaky peek through your F-hole." Dirty sod . . .

Strictly Come Dancing's stunning Erin Boag might have sounded like a shameless hussy, but she was talking about ballroom partners when she said: "I've had lots of big men."

Elizabeth Talbot, about to value an unused Chinese folding table on *Flog It!*: "Let's get it erected and we'll see what comes out at the end."

David Vine, talking about a female weightlifter at the Olympics: "This lady is magnificent, she already has a 158kg snatch under her belt." They just love the snatch references, these boys . . .

Ray Mears, discussing an Indonesian's lethal-looking machete on his BBC Bushcraft show: "With a weapon like this in my hand, I could do almost anything."

Former Gladiator Janie Omorogbe, talking about horse-riding to a startled novice: "Hold on tight, grip with your knees and let the animal do all the work." Wasn't that what Tiffany's mum told her when she married Grant Mitchell?

Emma Crowhurst, making jam with a fella on *Food and Drink*: "You've got quite big plums, I hope you don't mind me saying." Mind? Why should he mind?

Sarah Kennedy, discussing diction: "That's the trouble waking up at 2am and trying to get your tongue round things."

Pause For Sport V

John McEnroe, talking about Roger Federer's service at Wimbledon: "When Federer's wrist gets going, seeds are scattered all over SW19." Crikey!

David Lloyd, discussing cricket bat grips: "In the 60s, Clive Lloyd was so big he had to put on six or seven rubbers."

Sky Sports' golf commentator talking about an impressive shot at the PGA Championship: "Tiger Woods here, using his prodigious length to full effect."

Sue Barker, talking tennis: "When the balls are coming at her there's tremendous penetration."

Bruce Critchley, reporting from the Solheim Cup: "The arm up means Creamer is inside Laura Davies for the fifth time."

Nick Hallings, talking about an Atlas stone on *Britain's Strongest Man*: "It's amazing how quickly these big men can get it up."

Golf commentator Suzy Whaley, talking about a shot Stacy Prammanasudh was about to play: "I think she'd be happy with 12 inches." Who wouldn't?

Colin Jackson, on hurdler Bershawn Jackson: "He's blessed

with so much length speed, when he puts his foot down it responds immediately."

Rex Hunt, fishing for barramundi: "This isn't worth looking at but my mate's just pulled out a whopper."

David Seaman made a dramatic save during 2001's Arsenal v Chelsea match. As Sky's commentator noted: "Seaman's under it, ooh what a snatch!"

Volleyball insight from Eurosport's Matt Chilton: "As long as it's hard driven, you can splat with either palm." But it could make you go blind . . .

Tracey Austin, talking about a player's rapport with the Wimbledon crowd: "Amelie Mauresmo gives her supporters a little fist."

Clare Balding, discussing a horse's temperament on *Grandstand*: "He's what I call a dirty dog, he doesn't always put it all in." And that has to be frustrating . . .

Maureen Madill, talking about a golfer's drive at the *Women's Open*: "Sherri has a good healthy crack. Ken Brown will take a closer look at it."

Martin Brundle, talking about a driving manoeuvre at the European Formula 1 Grand Prix: "Massa slithers right up inside his team-mate."

Simon Golding, discussing Maria Mutola's efforts in the 800m on Eurosport: "It doesn't matter how hard she tries, she still has trouble pulling out a big one."

David Goldstrum fills us in on female weightlifters: "With an 85-kilo snatch, it's Russia's Elena Birshkis who's looking for a husband." Good luck with that . . .

Peter Alliss chatting to David Duval about golf: "He's pulled his ball back and given himself another three inches to play with."

Clayton Lucas, commenting on a Chinese beach volleyball player for Eurosport: "Wang, with all the knuckles round it, but he just can't get it up."

Michael Slater, anticipating a West Indies declaration on his BBC Test Match cricket coverage: "England players are waiting to see Jimmy Adams' hand pulling his batsmen off."

Hazel Irvine, talking to John Parrott about protracted play during the snooker final: "It looks as though we're in a grinding position now, John."

Goofs, Glorious Goofs II

Nicki Chapman had a go on an Austrian man's musical instrument on BBC1's *Holiday* show, and then goofed: "Oh, I think I've left some lipstick on his horn."

Kate Alcock on *Flog It!*, describing the cork in a wine bottle to a very surprised fella: "It's very long, hard and stiff, but if you bear with me I'd like to pull it off for you."

Kevin Ashman, talking about a local dish on BBC2's *Eggheads*: "I went to Guernsey last year but I didn't get round to eating any gache."

On *Loose Women*, Martine McCutcheon was asked what Michael Jackson would be remembered for. "How he touched people," she replied. You can say that again . . .

Richard Hammond, talking about a contender on BBC2's *Total Wipe-Out*, said: "She's a world-class athlete but even she couldn't handle those big red balls."

BBC weathergirl Louise Lear, admitting her mistakes to a shocked newsreader: "I have already had one big cock-up this morning."

Charlie Ross, inspecting a woman's cranberry-coloured

glassware on *Flog It!*: "I don't think I've ever seen such a large pair of pink jugs before."

The narrator describing tea being delivered door-to-door by horses on channel Five's *Disappearing Britain*: "Each horse is eager to deposit its aromatic load."

Tamzin Outhwaite, chatting about a bike she once got for Christmas on *EastEnders Fighting Fit*: "I found a purple chopper with a red bow wrapped round it waiting for me. I was thrilled." What girl wouldn't be?

Arlene Phillips, talking about Alesha Dixon's dance moves on BBC1's *Strictly Come Dancing*, goofed: "When Alesha's in a position, the going in and out can be a little bit clumsy." I find that very hard to believe . . .

Angela Harrison, talking to Neil Oliver on BBC2's *Coast* about selling wet fish: "From stiff to really floppy is not good."

Craig Revel Horwood, talking about Letitia Dean's feet on *Strictly Come Dancing*: "The balls were definitely stiffening during Letitia's performance."

The voiceover on BBC3's *Celebrity Scissorhands* lets us know about Rowetta Satchell's massage appointment: "In the beauty treatment room Rowetta is about to finish off her client, Bez." Sounds like a very happy Monday . . .

ITV weathergirl Emma Jesson, talking about combining work with being newly married: "I just fit it in when I can."

Gregg Wallace talking about Richard Arnold's cooking on *Celebrity Masterchef*: "He's pulled it out again and it's magnificent."

More Sporting Feet in Sporting Mouths

Sir Alex Ferguson: "I said it pre-season. In fact I may have said it before the season started."

Paul Merson: "Just two changes for Villa today, in come Osbourne, Davis and Baros."

John Inverdale: "The best horse won, and that's all you can say in any sport."

Rob McCaffrey: "Alan Curbishley is absolutely speechless, so what will he be saying at halftime?"

Peter Crouch on free kicks: "If you gave those all the time, you'd be giving them constantly."

BBC commentator Jake Humphrey: "Qualifying doesn't always tell us who has the quickest car, just who has the fastest car."

Andy Gray: "That goal is typical of Barcelona; it's just so un-Barcelona-like."

Arsene Wenger: "You can't recover from a European defeat. You recover from winning the next game."

Alan Mullery: "Defoe, Kanoute and Keane – they're looking like a great double act."

The Big Ones Keep Coming

That suave old smoothie Des Lynam was talking about doing impressions on Channel 4's *Countdown* when he revealed: "I can slip into Dale Winton anytime."

Linda Barker shocked Handy Andy on BBC1's *Changing Rooms* by remarking: "I'll just tidy this up and you can give me another twelve inches." You'll be lucky, love . . .

Chris Tarrant makes a shock revelation about £1million winner Judith Keppel on ITV's *This Morning*: "She was practising faster finger first by herself in bed last night." Blimey! If I'd seen that I would have definitely phoned a friend . . .

Well-endowed housemate Pete Bennett chatting to Big Brother about sexual attraction on the C4 show: "When you least expect it, it just pops up."

Here's Russell Brand talking about how tall he is: "My length is not apparent in the back of a cab." Which certainly makes a change . . .

Colin McAllister, discussing pre-wedding preparations on *Colin and Justin's Wedding Belles*: "The ladies-in-waiting are touching up the bride and everything's coming together."

Carol Vorderman, talking to Des O'Connor about contestants going for difficult number options on *Countdown*: "You love it when it's hard, don't you?" Well at his age, it can't happen very often, surely...

Serial goofer Ainsley Harriott told a teenage boy how to whisk eggs on *Ready Steady Cook*: "You have to keep beating it until it's stiff," he said, adding: "You'll learn."

A Sky newsreader startled viewers with this shock report in 2009: "A British soldier serving in Afghanistan has had a miraculous escape when a bullet passed straight through his helmet."

Gary Rhodes was commenting on a female guest preparing a fillet of fish when the spirit of the goof possessed him. "You've got a good eight inches in your hand and you're rolling it well," he said.

Comedian Mark Little advocated going meat-free for one day a week on channel Five's *The Wright Stuff*: "Once a week we should hide the sausage," he insisted. Well, it never hurt Dale Winton's career . . .

Charley Figgis filmed a report on commuting for BBC Newsroom South East and told viewers about her train journey. "Well, that's the first leg over and I'm already feeling hot," she said.

The Sport of Goofs

Dan Topolski, commentating on the World Rowing Championship: "Romania's men got a length, gave it 38 strokes a minute and were very solid by the end."

Vicki Butler Henderson, talking about laps at the British Touring Car Championship, asks a startled Gordon Shedden: "Will you be able to pop in a fast one this afternoon?"

Willie Thorne informs us about an Alan McManus snooker shot on *Grandstand*: "Alan needs an adrenalin surge through the balls."

Paul Dickenson, talking about Tyson Gay at the 100-metre athletics: "He's slow to rise, but Gay's stretched everyone with his all-comers record at Crystal Palace."

Colin Bryce, reporting from the Arnold Strongman Classic: "Pfister, three inches thick, up it goes a second time. Woah!" Steady on! He went on to say that Schwarzenegger himself was very impressed by it. I'm not at all surprised . . .

Graham Taylor, talking about Darren Campbell's pace upfront on Sky One soccer show *The Match*: "When Darren opens his legs he's a threat to anyone."

Golf expert Peter Allis, talking about Fijian legend Vijay Singh's driving iron: "Vijay has just pulled out his big tool."

Cricket commentator Tony Lewis on Kevin Dean's bowling: "He really should control his length and relax."

It's not all glamour on BBC Sport, you know. Jonathan Davies was helping out with the Rugby League Challenge Cup draw when he moaned: "This is what I've sunk to, holding people's ball bags." What a comedown!

Chris Hollins, commenting on Lewis Hamilton's victory in the Chinese Grand Prix: "Oh, and there's Hamilton's mother kissing him on the helmet."

Rod Harrington, describing Dennis Smith's throwing technique at the World Matchplay darts championship: "He takes it in his hand, rolls it between two fingers and then he gets a good release."

Wayne Grady, talking about Nick Faldo's tee-shot at the Open: "For a big strong man, Nick has never been as long as he should have been." Nature can play some cruel tricks . . .

Ian Wright, discussing the Spain v Tunisia game: "Fernando Torres had a right slash just outside the Tunisian penalty area." Messy bugger . . .

Tracey Austin, reporting from Wimbledon: "John McEnroe hasn't enjoyed two one-handers in a women's final since 1998."

John Motson, talking about the Brazilian football team: "They're so good it's like they're running around the pitch playing with themselves."

Goofs Galore IV

How should you clean a cow? Matt Baker enlightened thousands of *Blue Peter* viewers by telling us: "You have to rub the horn with baby oil."

Kirsty Gallacher, talking about the intermediary level of fences on BBC1 reality-TV show *Only Fools On Horses*: "It's risen by nine inches . . . I have to say it's rather large."

A male employee chatting about working with blue-movie producer Gary Kremanon on *The Sex.Com Story*: "Since I've been working with Gary, I have been hardened by porn."

On Channel 4's series *The Dark Side of Porn*, amateur film-maker Mandy asks her grandmother if she's ever seen any pornography. "Well," she replies, "I've seen a few snatches."

Alan Titchmarsh, discussing a Japanese cherry tree on *Ground Force*, informed us: "Remember, the more you stroke it the shinier it gets."

Bjorn Ulvaeous of Abba was talking about his lyrics on *TOTP 2* when he confided: "The girls hardly ever complained about anything, saying, 'I can't take this into my mouth.' That hardly ever happened."

BBC Breakfast weathergirl Louise Lear, talking about heavy overnight rain in the Southeast, informed us: "It woke me up a couple of times during the night. I had about an inch and a half." Which must have been disappointing . . .

Cat owner Julie was talking about exercising her tubby tabby on Sky 1's *Fat Pets* when she said: "I'm worn out playing with his balls while he just sits and relaxes."

Telly astrologer Russell Grant, talking about food rationing on ITV's *Fit Club*: "My mum always got a free sausage from the butcher. I remember it was very pink and it smelled nice." Vanessa Feltz was more impressed by the black pudding.

Cece Sammy, describing vocal technique to Mark and Natasha on *Just the Two of Us*: "Short and fat must become long and thin. You must keep doing it."

Jonathan Ross, finishing an interview with a startled Dustin Hoffman: "I'd like to hold you here and keep pumping you."

Jason Gardiner, discussing Stefan's convincing performance on ITV's *Dancing on Ice*: "If he gets to the final, he will pull it out . . . he always does."

When Melissa Porter showed a city dweller around a converted barn on *Escape To The Country*, the young girl took one look at the dining room and said: "It's very small, but I think it might go in long ways."

Here's Annabel Croft with a startling observation about a French tennis pro: "Amélie Mauresmo has a little snatch, and her forehead keeps getting tucked up in it."

Colin Bryce, commentating on the *Timber Sports World Series*, must have made ears prick up when he said: "Big Dale Ryan, huge chopper swinging away down by his feet."

Davina McCall, talking about the attraction between *Big Brother* inmates told Channel 4 viewers: "In the past few days we've seen something big start to grow between Faria and Dennis."

Bid-Up TV presenter Gerry McCullough, talking about adjusting an inflatable mattress: "During the night, sometimes you want it soft, and other times you want it hard." Hard is best, surely?

Shannon Ice was talking about a toy gun when she told David Letterman: "You have to do a lot of cocking and pumping before it shoots." Although knowing what we now know about the legendary Late Show presenter's love life, it can't have been surprising.

A grandad caught selling fake Viagra in a car park in Whitstable by BBC South East defended his actions. "I am not a hardened criminal," he said.

Vanessa Feltz, talking about packing a suitcase, disconcerted a poor bloke by asking: "Are you the sort who likes to shove it all in at once?" Like Vanessa does with a fresh cream gateau . . .

A US rollercoaster expert talking about the Stratosphere ride in Las Vegas on *Ultimate Coasters* revealed: "The girls are tied down, strapped up and prepared for a big thrust from underneath."

Tyra Banks, offering runway advice on *America's Next Top Model*: "You should walk as if there's wind blowing in your hair. You have to create your own wind." So, girls, always start the day with a bowl of prunes and some curried beans . . .

Pause For Sport VI

A frank confession from jockey Mick Fitzgerald about riding a horse in the Grand National: "I don't care what sex it is as long as I have one leg either side and I'm on top."

Colin Bryce gives a startling insight on *Britain's Strongest Man*: "If things weren't hard enough, contestants then have to erect a 250-kilo fisherman's pole." Lucky old fisherman . . .

Willie Carson was talking about a horse's reluctance to go into the stalls at Ascot when he opined: "A little pat on the backside and it goes straight in." Surely optimistic when said to Clare Balding?

Henry Blofeld, commentating on the last over at the second test: "It's all in Freddie Flintoff's hands now as he has five balls of his own." That explains the funny walk . . .

Nick Halling, explaining Jess Marunde's approach to the keg-toss event on *The World's Strongest Man*: "Some guys like to hold it long ways, others like it held horizontally, but Marunde's tossing them all like they weigh five kilos."

Gymnastics commentator Vincent Walduck raised a few eyebrows on Eurosport when he noted: "Ivankov – the arm muscle development is immense."

Bristol City manager Gary Johnson was talking about his physiotherapist subbing Adriano Basso when he said: "Our physio is only a small woman, and you wouldn't expect a small woman to be able to pull off a six-foot-four man."

John Inverdale stunned *Britain's Strongest Man* competitor Johnnie Kiss by asking: "Do you have to train to carry something of that magnitude between your legs?"

Scott Booth, commentating on a Dundee Utd v Rangers match, revealed: "Maurice Edu's taken out Goodwillie and the youngster's really feeling it."

Here's David Goldstrum, talking about Polish weigh-lifter Bartlomiej Bonk: "Bonk in the snatch . . . had 172 yesterday." Lucky sod!

Colin Bryce, commentating on Lindsay Alcock's Winter Olympics technique, informed us: "Alcock's blasting away with the one-handed technique, but it's quicker than two-handed." Which must have surprised a few people . . .

Colin Bryce again, talking about a 265lb weight on *The World's Strongest Man*: "The taller man has a bonus – he can swing it easier between his legs," later adding, "Six feet five, he can't even stand up without it bumping into his thighs."

Shaun Murphy, talking about his snooker comeback against Ken Doherty: "The wife has been monitoring my performance since the world championships and reckons I'm much better coming from behind."

Peter Alliss waxing lyrical about golfer Rodney Pampling: "He has played extremely well with his hands well down the grip and several inches of his shaft protruding."

Golf coach Butch Harmon demonstrating a shot on Sky Sports: "You need a little cock in your hand."

Cock-ups And Boobs

Erin Boag was demonstrating a dance move on BBC2's *Strictly Come Dancing: It Takes Two* when she told former EastEnders star Ricky Groves: "Open up your legs and I will come quickly between them." Bet Ricky was thinking the very same thing...

Who would have guessed Beatrice Hillyer was discussing the availability of fresh water in Baghdad when she informed TVam viewers: "Just after the liberation, I was getting it twice a day in my hotel room."

Sun journalist Sally Brockway got all flustered when she was chatting to Bruno Brookes about her hobby, Lambada dancing, on *Love At First Sight*. Sally told him: "I normally have ten partners every night."

Author Kingsley Amis was discussing critics on *Antenna* when he said: "I like a little poke now and then."

Here's an extraordinary statement from *Go Fishing*'s John Wilson, who said: "While I've got my rod out, let's have a look at the size of my waggler. I've got a 12-inch waggler." He meant his float, of course.

Comedian Miranda Hart was talking on *Strictly Come Dancing: It Takes Two* about Ian Waite being the only professional left who was tall enough to dance with her, when Craig Revell-Horwood chipped in: "Well, he has got the length of bone." If anyone would know, I'm sure Craig would.

On *Loose Women*, Andrea McLean revealed that her fiancée was flat on his back with an injury. Jane McDonald told her: "Let's hope he's upright for the honeymoon."

I bet this tickled a few old soldiers. During the Cenotaph ceremony on Remembrance Day, the BBC1 commentator said: "Leading the wreath bearers is trooper Mark Donaldson who ran eighty meters, exposing himself to the Taliban and won the Victoria Cross for his actions."

Kay Burley on *Sky News*, talking about superstar Madonna who had been out jogging in Central London: "Fans tried to get close to Madonna, only to be fended off by her bouncers." Let's chest hope she meant her bodyguards.

Anne Diamond had to introduce Hilary Jones on *TV Weekly*. "Here is the doctor half the women in Britain would love to be under," she said.

Carol Vorderman was talking about a number puzzle on *Countdown* when she told a stunned male contestant: "I can't wait to see the size of your big one."

The Sun's slimming queen Sally Ann Voak was referring to John Suchet's belly on *News At One* when she said: "I'm sure you have a little bulge down there, John."

A *Daytime Live* interviewer was chatting about a live production of Midsummer's Night Dream when she informed a delighted Roy Hudd: "I'll see your Bottom in Regent's Park this summer."

Over on *Ghosthunting with Louis Walsh & Boyzone* the Living TV voice-over informed us: "The very thought of entering Mary Jane's lower cavern is making Stephen Gately feel queasy." No further comment necessary.

Sue Barker raised eyebrows on BBC1's *A Question of Sport* when she told Phil Tufnell: "You've been so good on the floor lately I'm going to make it even harder for you." The minx!

Carry on Clanging – More Great Sporting Cock-ups

Golfer Sergio Garcia, talking about a four-man challenge at the World Cup tournament to commentator Tim Barter: "We love foursomes, we like playing with each other."

Ken Brown, talking about a golf club on *Live European Golf*: "David Howells has a wand in his hand, 32 inches long and he knows how to use it." Lucky Mrs Howells . . .

Gymnastics expert Christine Still gets quite carried away on BBC2 at times. Here she is commentating on the men's vault: "Draguiescu has the most tremendous length. The Romanian is so huge he can insert two twists in it and still reach the end of the mat with it." Blimey.

Andy Gray, talking about Man United's tight defence: "Silvestre was in Joe Cole's pants trying to win the ball."

Mike Tucker reporting from the Badminton Horse Trials: "Matthew Wright's coming home hard, and if he looks down he'll see he's getting just the sort of ride Polly Stockton would like."

Pam Shriver, informing millions of Wimbledon viewers: "If

that ball had gone between Agassi's legs he would have pulled out a beauty."

Ian Payne talking tennis: "Anna Kournikova stands with legs wide apart, and gets ready to receive."

Peter Drury commentating on the Boat Race, drew our attention to "Kip McDaniel, the feeler of the Cambridge crew's rhythm and their cox."

Richard Pitman reporting from the Grand National said: "Tony McCoy's oiled his body, Peter Scudamore's ridden him and tells me he's in magnificent condition."

Sam Torrance, asking Ernie Els about golf drives at Wentworth's World Matchplay: "What's Angel Cabrera's length compared to yours?"

Peter Alliss on Rivero's golf drive: "Gosh, what an enormous one for such a little chap!"

Jon Champion, commentating on the Women's Cup Final: "Jordan Nobbs, the youngest member of Sunderland's youth team . . ." What a lucky lad.

Geoff Boycott, talking about fielding around Shane Warne: "What he wants is a man right up his backside." Each to his own . . .

Graham Taylor, talking about Djibril Cisse's running speed during the Liverpool v Sofia match: "If he opens his legs he's hard to handle."

Garry Herbert, commentating on the world rowing contest: "It's very exciting to see two women get hold of a length and come together in a boat."

INNUENDO BONANZA!

Golf legend Peter Allis, talking about Paul Casey's opening shot on the first tee at the British Open: "Now he *has* got an enormous length."

John Watson, remarking to Graham Le Saux about lofty England footballer Peter Crouch's heading ability on BBC1: "I wonder if he's got anything below as well." Ask Abigail Clancy . . .

Wayne Grady reporting on the golf: "Retief Goosen's fiddled with his shaft – a little thing but it can make a big difference."

Willie Carson, talking about the going a racehorse prefers – that's the course condition for non-enthusiasts - told Clare Balding: "He likes it firm with a good rattle coming from his feet." Don't we all?

David Corkill, commentating on the Indoor Bowls World Championship: "Jonathan Ross has got a length of one inch to jack . . . and he's a front toucher."

Clive Everton, talking about Shaun Murphy's rest during his match against Matthew Stevens in the Snooker World Championship Final: "Players normally have a four-inch or five-inch extension, but Matthew has this extra-long one."

Jockey Graham Lee, talking about riding at Cheltenham for the first time to Clare Balding: "I came here as a virgin jockey and the good rides I've had over the four days have left me exhausted."

Matt Chilton was commentating on the World Rowing Championship 2009 for Eurosport when he informed viewers: "Long, powerful Eric Murray is stroking the New Zealander's semi while Hamish Bond is just sitting there."

Jonathan Davies, describing a Gavin Henson rugby tackle during the Scotland v Wales Six Nations match: "That's the perfect tackle when he lifts his leg and dumps!" *Can his other half, Charlotte Church please confirm?*

And the Goofs Go on

Cuddly game lord Dale Winton was talking about his holding pen for losers on *In It to Win It*, when he told a startled contestant: "Let's have a look at my red area," he said. Hussy.

And here's another belter from the wanton Winton. Dale was waiting for the answer to where a sou'wester is worn when he told startled viewers: "I'm looking for head."

Goof-lover Dale tells me the prudish BBC left his best ever *In It To Win It* clanger on the edit suite floor, but at least the studio audience had a good laugh when he announced: "I'm looking for eight inches." Not for the first time . . .

Len Goodman was talking about kneecaps on *Strictly Come Dancing: It Takes Two*, when he told a startled Claudia Winkleman: "You've got a very bony knob there and your bony knob should be just behind my bony knob."

Jennifer was cooking coq au vin on *Two Fat Ladies* when Clarissa remarked: "There's a lot of good in an old cock, isn't there?" I'd say so.

David Dickinson, discussing some fine Victorian fur hand-warmers on *Dealing with Dickinson*: "Ladies had big muffs in those days."

Lorne Spicer, chatting about a saxophone to Mark Franks on *Car Booty*: "I'm blowing hard but I can't get anything out of it."

Anne Robinson, with regard to an answer on *The Weakest Link,* announced rather grandly: "I will accept Dick." But is there a man alive that brave?

BBC Breakfast weathergirl Helen Young recently warned viewers about high winds and rain: "You'll find it hard to keep it up today." She was, of course, talking about your umbrellas, folks . . .

Phil Tufnell was shown how to winkle a cricket out of its nest with a small piece of grass, on BBC1's *The One Show*. "They don't like things being poked in their holes," he observed. Who does? Apart from Dale obviously.

Jeff Stelling was clearly impressed by co-host Rachel Riley's outfit on Channel 4's long-running *Countdown*: "You're looking very nautical tonight," he told her. "Fancy spending an hour on my vessel later?"

Dr Glenn Wilson, talking about a scoring device on BBC1's *Secrets of the Sexes* observed: "Well, the knob has gone up a little bit there, so she obviously likes him." (And presumably vice versa?)

Jenny Barnett may have been talking about butter on *Good Food Bites*, when she asked chef Gino D'Acompo: "How big is your knob?" Brazen.

Have BBC News 24 got no compassion? "And now the news in brief," said the announcer, and they flashed up a photo of Saddam Hussein in his underpants.

Adrian Chiles was talking to Miss Scotland about her coming from the same town as tennis pro Andy Murray on BBC1's *The One Show* when he asked, "Did he ever give you a good knock up?"

David Goldstrom, commentating on Kate Lawler's fighting techniques on ITV's short-lived *Celebrity Wrestling*: "Brawler trying the same wrist action . . . Inferno jerking her off."

The wonderfully named Zoe Hardman was talking about the male contenders' good qualities on *Playing It Straight*: "They've all got little things that are lovely," she said.

Mark Franks, discussing an expanding dinner table on *Sun, Sea and Bargain Spotting*: "When you pull it out it gets bigger and wider, but when you push it back in it collapses like a concertina."

Contestant Jasmine was talking about an acting challenge on Bravo's *Make Me a Supermodel* when she said: "It seemed a lot bigger than it was, but it actually came quite easily."

Lorne Spicer, discussing kitchenware on *Cash In The Attic*: "Let's go downstairs, where Julie is happily showing her jugs to Mark."

Ben Fogle, when asked by a TV reporter what effect rowing the Atlantic naked would have on his body, very honestly admitted: "It's unlikely to be a big thing."

Did They Really Say That?

Sir Alex Ferguson: "We've only got two and a half days to prepare, so that's 72 hours."

Ray Domenech: "I don't believe in superstitions, they bring bad luck."

Classic clanger from Greg Norman: "I owe a lot to my parents, especially my mother and father."

Phil Neville: "I've never been so certain about anything in my life. I want to be a coach. Or a manager. I'm not sure which."

Neal Foulds on snooker wiz Ally Carter: "He has been in the final of this tournament before and people often go on from there to win it."

BBC Wimbledon commentator 2009: "Yes, the wind is coming from Federer's end."

Barry McGuigan: "It wasn't a comeback, I always intended to come back."

Chris Kamara: "Sheffield United-Ipswich will be an open game, but I think the team that scores the most goals will win tonight."

Clive Tyldesley: "England are learning to walk before they can run with their feet nailed firmly to the ground."

Gordon McQueen: "One thing Alex Ferguson didn't want – injuries and suspensions."

Paul Merson: "None of the Moscow players appealed, in fact one of them did."

Clive Tyldesley: "Free kick to Preston . . . just how fatal will it be for Liverpool?" Well if the ball were packed with explosives...

More Sporting Feet in Mouths II

Gordon McQueen on Alex Ferguson: "He's got one eye on the league, one eye on Europe and another eye on what's going on in the boardroom."

Phil Neville: "We're on the top of the cliff now, so we either fall off or keep climbing."

Ian McCall: "It will probably be nil-nil, but you'll definitely see goals today."

John Motson: "Buffon hasn't had time to shake hands with anyone, apart from every one of his team mates."

David Pleat: "It looked a little bit worse than it appeared."

John Champion: "Fact is of Arsenal's 56 goals, Thierry Henry's scored only 12 of them." Big Ron: "Yeah, but he created the other 40."

Andy Croxall: "Aston Villa attacking their 1,000 plus fans behind the goal."

Murray Walker "Oh, and Mansell can see him in his earphone!"

Andy Gray: "There are a lot of tired legs in those white

shirts."

Geoffrey Boycott: "The England bowlers have got a mountain to climb on this flat pitch."

Roger Federer: "In tennis there has to be a winner sometimes."

Paul Masefield: "Ronaldo can pull anything out of the hat at the drop of a whim."

Another classic from Brian Johnston: "Fred Titmus has two short legs, one of them square."

Jamie Redknapp: "There's no reason why Anelka and Drogba can't play together in that role, although Drogba's now suspended so they can't."

Goofs Galore V

A great gaffe from Seabird Centre spokesman Richard Yeddon, quoted on The One Show: "Our bird expert George has rescued a variety of seabirds recently including gannets and gulls, but he hasn't had a shag for weeks."

A determined WPC talking about a man seen flashing on a train, on *Rail Cops*: "We're looking for a pervert with an erect penis and when we find him we're going to pull him off." How jolly decent of her!

Richard Whiteley, asking Susie Dent about the validity of a word on Countdown, enquired: "Nookie, is that OK with you Susie?" I'd be amazed if it wasn't . . .

Clare Balding was talking about a Horse Guard's drum at the Lord Mayor's Show on BBC1, and praising his "magnificent beast". "It takes a lot of practice to handle," he said proudly. "I know," she replied. "I've seen you at it in Hyde Park."

Screen legend Joan Collins, discussing Elton John's union jack ring on *GMTV*: "Elton's always been a great ring man." No one has ever doubted that . . .

Christopher Biggins, talking about filming schedules for blue movies on *Sex in the '70s*: "It was a bit like doing a soap opera now, there were no rehearsals; it was just in and out."

Cheeky comic Bradley Walsh, plugging his new DVD, told Des O'Connor how he once met Princess Michael of Kent: "I tried to slip her one, but she wasn't having none of it." He meant the DVD, of course.

Over on Channel 4 *Wife Swap* hunting enthusiast Glen hadn't shared a bed with his wife for 11 years. As the voiceover helpfully explained, "To relieve tension, Glen loves nothing more than to shoot his guns and mount his animals."

Sexy Catherine McQueen, talking about getting soaked in a *Simply the Best* water game on ITV: "I'm wet already, so I'm ready for anything."

Asked how old he was, a *Countdown* contestant told Richard Whiteley he was 69 and retired. "That's a nice position to be in," goofed Richard.

Jane McDonald, asking chef James Martin about a cake he'd brought on to *Loose Women*: "How do you get it so big and moist? Is it all in the wrist?"

Dr Zahi Hawass, commenting on his excavation plans on *Golden Mummy Tomb Opening Live*: "The mummy's been sealed up for thousands of years, so I'm going to enter her with my tools." Dr Hawass has "had his down some of the dirtiest mummy shafts in Egypt," according to Kate Sanderson.

Richard Park, talking about Ewan McGregor's skill with the French horn on *Greatest TV Wannabe Moments*: "He's fantastic at everything he does and I think that probably just about includes the horn."

Here's Gabby Logan, asking a female contestant about scuba diving on ITV's *The Vault*: "Do you still get excited at the thought of going down?"

Derek Thompson, explaining background noises to Emma Ramsden on *The Morning Live*: "There's a lot of carefree banging going on here at Newcastle."

British voice-over man Howard Hughes, discussing *Emmerdale* stunner Malandra Burrows' building skills on ITV's *Simply the Best*, observed: "Malandra's handiwork can have your extension up in no time." I don't doubt it . . .

Matt Willis, talking about Jason Donovan's camp task on *I'm a Celebrity*: "Who gets wood first thing in the morning with Jason?" Scott Henshall, I should imagine . . .

Medium Derek Acorah, squealing excitedly about being possessed by the spirit of Lord Sackville on *Most Haunted*: "He's a big man, very big; he's attempting to enter me. He's towering over me and could probably give me another six inches yet." Tsk, Derek, and you a married man as well.

A concerned Philip Schofield was discussing Leslie Grantham's off-screen sexploits on *This Morning* with Tracy-Ann Oberman, who played Dirty Den's soap wife Chrissie, when he asked: "So are the rest of the cast all pulling together?"

Paul Martin, talking to a taxidermist about stuffing pet animals on *Flog It!*: "No matter how well they're mounted, they never have the expression on their faces that their owners remember."

Sir Roy Strong, discussing David Bailey's pictures on *Fame, Fortune and Photography*: "What took me by surprise were the nudes. I remember thinking, 'Who's going to swallow that?'"

Own Goals – More Great Sporting Goofs

Here's the ever reliable Mike Tucker reporting from the Hickstead Derby: "18 inches makes a huge psychological difference for riders when they're going into that mesmerising dyke." I should say so . . .

Gavin Peacock, commentating on Chelsea goalie Carlo Cudicini: "Cudicini had a soft one between the legs, but Chelsea pulled it out for him at the end of the game."

Sports commentator Andrew Jameson got rather excited during the mens' 100 metres butterfly (Summer Olympics): "Crocker has some very big men inside him," he gasped. "And oh, there's Mankoc in lane eight." That's Slovenian swimming sensation Peter Mankoc of course.

Voice-over on *Grand Prix Nazi*, a Channel 4 documentary about racing driver Richard Seaman: "The Fuehrer approved of Dick so there was no turning back. Dick Seaman loved the Germans and the Germans loved Dick Seaman."

Cricket expert David Lloyd, commentating on the 2006 Ashes: "Brett Lee's found his length, swinging it massively. Umpire Bucknor stands firm."

'Not up' is a technical term for a tennis ball that double bounces, which is why Virginia Wade assured Wimbledon fans: "The player always knows when they've got it up."

Staying at Wimbledon, Sue Barker was talking about a service: "Andy Roddick whips out that weapon and bangs it in at 150 miles an hour. I would love to know how that feels."

On Sky1's *The Match*, Alesha Dixon then from R&B group Mis-Teeq chatted about the way husband to be MC Harvey pulled his shirt over his head after scoring a goal: "If Harvey scores he'll definitely be doing some shirt-lifting," she said.

Here's golfer Luke Donald, talking about holing his final putt in his Ryder Cup doubles match: "It was a knee-trembler, but luckily I got my stroke right and it went straight in."

Nick Halling, commentating on *The World's Strongest Man*: "Glenn Ross, tools at arms' length . . . Terry Hollands gets hold of it, moves it, wobbles it; but in the end just plays with it."

Luke Sutton, posing a cricket question: "Who would you most like to see down under tossing Ricky Pointing? It's Andrew Flintoff, isn't it?"

Millwall FC's Adrian Serioux, commenting on his famously long throw-in: "I'd like to think I have one of the biggest around. I can ping it right on someone's head if I want."

Alan Mullery, discussing Ipswich strikers Darren and Marcus Bent: "With the Bent guys on top they have every chance of coming from behind."

Andy Jameson, commentating on the World Swimming Championships: "Popov's got Ian Thorpe behind him, straining to put everything into his back end."

What a Carry On!

Filthy innuendo has been a cornerstone of British humour for hundreds of years, and audiences always enjoy lapping it up. Geoffrey Chaucer employed it as long ago as the 14th century. In *The Canterbury Tales*, 'The Wife of Bath's Tale' is littered with delicious double meanings, the most famous being her use of the old word 'queynte' to talk about her quaint domestic duties and her private parts – queynte being the old English root of the vulgar Anglo-Saxon c***.

Shakespeare loved a double entendre too. Sir Toby Belch in *Twelfth Night* says of Sir Andrew's hair, "it hangs like flax on a distaff, and I hope to see a housewife take thee between her legs and spin it off." Hamlet winds up Ophelia with 'country' puns, while time is told in *Romeo and Juliet* with the phrase "for the bawdy hand of the dial is now upon the prick of noon."

In *Much Ado about Nothing*, Benedick is clearly talking about a condom when he says, "a whole bookful of those quondam carpet mongers . . . were never so truly turned over and over as my poor self in love . . . I can find out no rhyme to *lady* but *baby* . . . for *scorn horn,* a hard rhyme."

The British Music Hall reveled in the low art of innuendo

too. Marie Lloyd famously sang, 'She Sits among the Cabbages and Peas', and the tradition passed on via Max Miller and Benny Hill, even finding a middleclass voice in Humphrey Lyttleton – who was dubbed the "purveyor of blue-chip filth to middle England". On the long-running hit radio show, I'm Sorry I Haven't a Clue, Littleton created the fictional scorer Samantha who had a particularly busy private life. "Samantha is a croupier," he revealed. "And often works at an exclusive Soho club where gamblers pay top money to play roulette all day and poker all night."

She also once trained opera singers – "having seen what she did to the baritone, the director is keen to see what she might do for a tenor." While her baking chef "popped her bread rolls straight into his mouth and he's promised to try her muffin next week."

The innuendo has flourished wherever sexuality is repressed and prudishness grips the country's moralists. No surprise then to find double meanings flourishing in Polari (Britain's gay underground slang), along with euphemisms. In radio comedy *Round the Horn*, gay characters Julian and Sandy had "a criminal practice that takes up much of our time." They could be found 'doing' the Gas Board, or in a spoof ad Julian was "stood there with it fizzing in me hand."

Gay comic Julian Clary has made a career out of 'tight passage' gags since the 1980. In his latest Edinburgh show, Julian reminisces, "I did *Two Gentlemen of Verona* here in 1984 . . . They said they were from Verona, anyway." In describing an imagined cigarette commercial, Julian claimed, "I'd take a puff and ride off."

For all of us who grew up in the 60s and 70s, however, the *Carry On* films represent the high point of the double meaning in popular culture. Although hated by TV liberals who briefly banned them from our screens in the late 80s, the movies always struck a chord with the public. Largely you suspect because they blew a resounding raspberry at authority figures and middle class kill-joys. George Orwell's famous essay celebrating the postcards of Donald Gill applies equally to these films.

Here *Carry On* legend Barbara Windsor – always a great fan of 'Garry's Goofs' – picks her guide to the Top Ten best-ever gags from those wonderful, innuendo-packed movies:

Kenneth Williams as Julius Caesar: "Infamy, infamy! They've all got it in for me!" (*Carry on Cleo*)

The Khasi of Kalabar (Kenneth Williams): "May the great god Shivoo bring blessings on your house." Sir Sidney Ruff-Diamond (Sid James): "And on yours." The Khasi: "And may his radiance light up your darkness." Sidney: "And up yours!" (*Carry on up the Khyber*)

Kenneth Williams: "Why me? You can have Tom, Dick or Harry." Suzanne Danielle: "But I don't want Tom and Harry." (*Carry on Emmanuelle*)

Matron (Hattie Jacques): "Young chickens may be soft and tender but older ones have more meat on them." Sid James: "True, and they take a lot more stuffing." (*Carry on Doctor*)

June Whitfield refuses a drink and smoke because she "tried them once and didn't like it." Sid James: "Odd." June: "Not at all . . . my daughter is just the same." Sid: "Your only daughter,

I presume." (*Carry on Abroad*)

Kenneth Williams: "You may not realise it but I was once a weak man." Hattie Jacques: "Once a week is enough for any man." (*Carry on Doctor*)

Kenneth Williams: "It's an enigma. That's what it is, Matron, an enigma!" Sid James: "I'm not having another one of them." (*Carry on Doctor*)

Detective Sergeant Bung (Harry H Corbett): "We can't afford to leave any stone unturned. What's the name of this road, Slobotham?" DC Slobotham (Peter Butterworth): "Er, Avery Avenue, sir." Bung: "Well, like I said, we must explore Avery Avenue." (*Carry on Screaming*)

Captain Potts (Eric Barker): "**Your rank!**" James Bailey (Kenneth Williams) "That's a matter of opinion!" *(Carry On Sergeant)*.

Charlie Roper (Sid James): "I dreamt about you last night, nurse." Nurse Sandra May (Barbara Windsor): "Did you?" Roper: "No, you wouldn't let me." (*Carry on Doctor*)

Good old Barbara. She did *Carry on Camping* because she really loved camping, *Carry on Spying* because she really liked spy films and *Carry on Dick* 'cos she really . . . had a thing about highwaymen.

Good Sports, Bad Goofers

David Corkhill, commentating on a particularly close bowls match on BBC2: "John Leeman has ten inches to play on his forehands, but he'll find Les Gillett a very hard man to shake."

Mike Tucker, reporting from the Badminton Horse Trials, was talking about a jockey and her peculiarly named horse, when he said: "Here comes Kitty Baggis, who is riding Five Boys in the open arena, and the grooms are all joining in with her mum 'cos it's a real family affair."

Here's Sam Torrance, talking about golfers' positions on the green during the Matchplay Gold: "Lee Westwood's inside Goosen with his putter and he can make those three or four inches hurt." And the eyes water?

The triple jump is fraught with problems, but I wasn't the only one who was surprised to hear Jonathan Edwards say: "Ashia Hansen had a cock-up just before the board and only put in 13.2 metres."

John McEnroe, talking about Andy Murray at Wimbledon, insisted: "He needs to do away with that between the legs play."

Here's Peter Alliss discussing golf clubs at the Open: "If you have a big head on a long shaft, sometimes they're difficult to control . . ." So I'd imagine . . .

John Parrott, commenting on a Ronnie O'Sullivan shot at the Grand Prix Snooker Final: "He got a big kick and both balls were off the table on connection." Ouch!

Howzat! Mike Atherton describes the condition of a used cricket ball during the England/New Zealand Test coverage: "English balls are generally a much better shape and not as shiny as the ones you get in India and Australia."

Tennis ace Pat Cash, talking about Karlovic's amazing service: "When it's going into the body it needs to be hard and fast, preferably both."

And here's Pat discussing return services during BBC2's tennis coverage: "Put balls straight down her neck and Kim Clijsters will keep coming all day." Which must be exhausting . .

Andrew Castle, reporting from the French Open tennis: "Coria, two short balls, but he'll keep massaging them until Henman's covered.

Jim McGrath, chattering about the stamina of a horse called Norse Dancer on *Channel 4 Racing*: "He has a little bit more between his legs and he's pounding away well." Bless . . .

Angus Loughran, discussing pole-vaulter Yelena Isinbeyeva's performance: "She wants him to keep inching and inching and inching it up, with Sergei doing the measuring."

Gary Pallister, talking about Chris Sutton's footballing techniques during an 'Old Firm' Rangers v Celtic match on BBC1: "Sutton likes to feel you against him, he loves the physical side and likes to get in that hole."

Anne Jones, discussing Danny Sapsford at Wimbledon as a note of disappointment enters her voice. "Danny has temporarily lost his length." Which is always disconcerting...

Goofs Galore VI

The Home & Leisure channel's continuity announcer, talking about fishing informed the listening dozens: "And next we have Henry Gilbey, who'll be dipping his tackle into Devon waters."

Pop Idol man mountain Rik Waller was discussing competing against the magnificent Josie D'Arby on *Back to Reality* when he opined: "Anyone who comes up against Josie is going to have it hard." I don't doubt it.

I don't normally include scripted lines as goofs, but *Neighbours* made me laugh back in 2000. Talking about Tad fancying another guy's girl, Flick said: "It's a big hot sweaty love triangle." At least that's what we've all heard . . .

Colin McAllister, talking about how to maximise the space in your house on the BBC's *Trading Up*: "Now we're in the bedroom where an extra couple of inches can make all the difference."

Carol Smillie, discussing impersonating a fella on Channel 4's *Gender Swap* confided: "I can't imagine being able to pull off a guy I didn't like." Just grit your teeth and think of Scotland, love.

Here's channel Five's *House Doctor*'s interior decorator, Ann

Maurice, talking about painting: "A quick lick or two can freshen up your entrance."

Colin McAllister, advising us about doors on the BBC's *Trading Up*: "Pay a bit of attention to your knob to make it stand out."

Des O'Connor was chatting away about getting girlfriend Jodie pregnant when he told his Des & Mel co-host Mel Sykes, "I feel all floppy now." Must have taken it out of him, the poor old soul . . .

Justin Ryan, talking about doing up a lounge on *Trading Up*: "Gavin's next door with Claire going at it hammer and tongs."

Anna Ryder-Richardson, the Duchess of DIY, talking to handymen Phil and JJ on *House Invaders*: "I'm going to check out the bedroom while you two get your tools out."

Fred Dibnah, at the coalface of a mine on the BBC's *Dig with Dibnah*, came out with this extraordinary statement: "I've got the girth," he said. "So you don't slew away from the wall when you're banging away."

Paul Martin, introducing antiques expert Charlie Ross on *Flog It!*: "Charlie tees off with an ancient club and an equally old pair of balls."

An extraordinary claim from Emma Kennedy, commentating on *The Other Boat Race*: "If Jonathan Aitken starts coxing aggressively and keeps coming at her, Konnie Huq won't be able to keep her head."

Roger Black, trying to guess the correct meaning of a word with possible connections to France on *Call My Bluff*, admitted:

"I'm not very good with French letters."

Richard Whiteley, summing up the scores on *Countdown*: "69 and 69, that's an interesting position. Let's see what happens next!"

Anna Ryder Richardson, pointing out AA Milne characters on *Whose House?*: "There's Tigger on the wall, and look there's Pooh on the bed."

The delightful Jenny Powell was talking about nothing naughtier than grammatical phrases on ITV game show *Wheel of Fortune* when she said: "I like a variety of lengths."

Here's saucy Cindy Beale actress Michelle Collins, discussing festive singles on *The Christmas Show*: "I really like the new Darkness one, I dunno the title, it's something about a bell end." It was 'Christmas Time (Don't Let the Bells End)', Michelle – but we like your version better.

Nick O'Dwyer, talking to two housewives about hygiene on *Rat Attack,* said: "You look like ladies who like to keep a nice clean back passage." Cheeky!

Deal or No Deal competitor Steven O'Donnell had a shock confession to make: "I can feel something big and red in my box, Noel," he claimed.

Paul Ross, making an eye-watering revelation about some edited film footage on ITV's *This Morning*: "Ewan McGregor had his 'dangly bits' hanging out, but this won't be shown in the US as they have been sliced." Ouch.

David Barby, talking to a woman on *Flog It!* about pouring vessels: "What a fabulous pair of jugs!"

BBC1's *Big Strong Boys* were trying to get a roll of floor covering through a window when Jake said, "I think you'll have to bend it to get it in," and Gavin protested, "It's as far in as I can push it."

And here are some more risky sounding DIY instructions from Jake: "Put your hand there, and your knee there, and I'll screw from the other side."

Pause For Sport VII

Tennis pro turned commentator John Lloyd served up this puzzling summary from the Australian Open: "Tim Henman spent the entire set thinking about big ones with his forehand," he said.

A question from BBC2's gymnastics expert Christine Still: "Can you imagine the pressure on the men's ring when they lower themselves into that Broom Handle?" Well I can, but if it's all right with you, Chris, I'd rather not.

Martin Brundell, looking for celebrities to interview in the crowded pits at the Monaco Grand Prix, told viewers: "I think I'll just take a chance and have a poke in the middle."

Here's Peter Alliss talking about a club on Live Golf: "Colin Montgomerie can take out his wood, and it's still longer than some of the younger players."

Paul Dickenson, was commentating on a wonderfully-named contestant on *The World's Strongest Man* when he said: "Pfister in the centre, pushing hard."

Willie Thorne, holding forth on cleanliness at the UK Snooker Final: "I never like my balls cleaned with white gloves, I prefer them given a good rub with a wet cloth."

Over at the Olympics Steve Cram was busy commentating on the 10,000 metres when he claimed: "The Ethiopians came out hard and they've been pulling away ever since," he said.

Sky Sport's Andy Gray was discussing a shot by Man United's Norwegian striker Ole Gunnar **Solskjær** when he made what could have been mistaken for a shocking libel: "If he'd gone across Nigel Martyn he'd have found a big gap for a little bender," he said.

Tim Caple, reporting from the Women's Football World Cup, observed: "I can't remember a tournament where there's been less balls in the area."

Martina Navratilova, making an extraordinary claim at Wimbledon: "If there's one thing that Serena Williams loves, it's whipping her opponents all over."

After hitting a record-breaking round of 64, golfer Richard Johnson told *Sunday Grandstand*: "If someone had offered me a 69 this morning, I would have taken it." Well, it's the best way to start the day.

Colin Bryce, commentating on arm-wrestling for Eurosport: "Big men, lots of sweating, Paul's bent over, Arthur's well-pumped, and then the referee gets the strap-on."

Eurosport commentator Simon Golding was talking about the effect of rain on the female beach volleyball teams when he told us: "What you can see there are some very wet Brazilians with nothing left between their legs except jelly."

Gourmet Gaffes- Cooking and Cock-Ups

Too many chefs may spoil the broth (and the telly) but as long as they carry on serving up goofs I'm happy to put up with them....

Here's a verbatim quote from *Celebrity Masterchef*'s Gregg Wallace: "Sally Gunnell, the tart didn't look appetising." That was a bit uncalled for . . .

Rick Stein, explaining a recipe on his *Food Heroes*: "Once placed in the oven your little balls will swell in size." Maybe, but would you risk it, fellas?

Here's pukka f..., uh, fella, Jamie Oliver discussing the art of whipping eggs: "I have to go through the pain barrier till it's nice and stiff," he said. "But you can be quite rough with it."

French chef Yvan Cadou shocked Fern Britton on *Ready Steady Cook* by revealing: "It's very exciting to get inside the bird." He may have been talking about quail . . .

The heavenly Nigella Lawson, discussing making the dough for cakes on *Nigella Bites*: "I usually start it by hand and I certainly finish it off by hand."

Here's an absolute belter; the voice-over guy on *Rosemary*

Shrager's School For Cooks informed viewers: "Both teams are boning like pros." They must have learned that from Gordon Ramsay and Sarah Symonds...

Voice-over man Dave Lamb was talking about a female contestant's likely reaction to an alcohol-laced dessert on Channel 4 *Come Dine With Me* when he pondered: "I wonder if she'll appreciate a stiff little surprise in the bottom."

More Random Goofs

Tony Blair, describing his wife on *The Real Cherie Blair*: "She's a giver not a taker." There's an image I'd rather not conjure with . . .

A woman arrested for shoplifting in Manchester was found to have an entire salami in her knickers, according to BBC News North West. When asked why she replied that she was missing her Italian boyfriend.

Justin Ryan, talking about decorating on *Trading Up*, said of his gay partner Colin McAllister: "Colin and Judy are hard at it in the pink bedroom." Well, there's a first time for everything.

And here's Colin McAllister, talking about renovating an old table on the same show: "Once you get the top off and separate the legs, you're home and dry." Like he'd know . . .

Medium Derek Acorah was feeling the psychic vibes along the balcony of a historic Welsh inn where criminals were once executed. Ashen-faced, he told his *Most Haunted* team: "This is where they tossed people off."

A husband describing his wife's pleasure on the appallingly titled *D.I.Why?* confided: "I've not seen her that happy since I did the tongue in groove on the staircase."

Here's Judy Finnegan, dreamily reminiscing about '70s Xmas toys: "There's a brand new chopper behind the settee just itching to be ridden."

Esther Rantzen was discussing muggers when she said: "You'd never think you could get them out in broad daylight on a busy street like this."

Jessica Holm, talking about a pedigree dog breeder at Crufts, informed viewers: "Alan Webster has been in cocker spaniels for 35 years and his bitch is performing brilliantly given the huge entry."

Phil Vickery was showing his missus Fern Britton how to make pancakes on *This Morning* when he told her: "The stiffer it is, the easier it is to toss."

Penny Smith, talking about an accident she had with a door on *GMTV*, revealed: "I was in agony, it was such a big knob and very painful."

Jasmine Lowson, commenting about a lorry driver on *Dumber and Dumber*: "With the excitement of the chase the driver spills his load all over the highway."

Foot in Mouth IV

Kate Thornton paying tribute to the just deceased movie star Patrick Swayze on *Loose Women:* "When you look back at those clips, you realise that Patrick Swayze was one of a dying breed." Oh dear.

Sky Sports' Gerry Armstrong: "Pinpoint accuracy there from Beckham. Two inches lower and that would have been a goal."

Steve Cram demonstrating his powers of observation: "Watching Usain Bolt you have to keep one eye on the race, one eye on the athlete and one eye on the result."

Glenn Hoddle, also on Sky Sports: "Chelsea have five or six injured players out at the moment and if Ashley Cole is injured that makes it seven or eight."

ITN's Robert Moore, was reporting on the Republicans' successes in the US mid-term elections: "George Bush will be savouring the victory of his fruits."

Matt Jackson: "Roy Keane, a personification of himself, in a way."

A propos his appearance on Who Do You Think You Are, *This Morning* presenter Fern Britton asked Chris Moyles: "Did your great-grandfather have any children?"

Geoff Boycott: "I only watch the replays afterwards."

Carlton Kirby of Eurosport: "Two Spanish flags for the crowd to see – one of them Japanese."

Brian Johnston: "Neil Harvey's at slip, with his legs wide apart, waiting for a tickle."

Graham Taylor: "Of course mistakes are made. Some are even accidental."

Pause For Sport VIII

Here's Eurosport legend Simon Golding commentating on women's beach volleyball: "The Brazilians are exposed and Wang's quickly up in the air." You can see why it's popular . . .

Mick Tucker, reporting from the Badminton Trials: "Lucinda Fredericks, a great ride, and if I had Lucinda wrapping her long legs around me I think I'd jump around like a little horse."

Dennis Taylor, discussing Stephen Hendry's snooker dominance: "Balls on the table, Hendry scoring well, opening up Ronnie O'Sullivan . . ."

Golf commentator Peter Alliss, complaining about the lack of long hitters during the third round of the US Masters, told us: "The leader board is filled with men of modest length."

Racing commentator Dave Smith, talking about Frankie Dettori romping home on Zelanda without a challenger in sight: "And Dettori looks between his legs and there's nothing there." Poor Frank . . .

Here's Tony Hawks talking about coxswains at the University Boat Race: "For top class cox, size and weight is crucial." So I've heard . . .

Alex Hay was discussing golf clubs when he came up with this intriguing statement: "Tinkering with his wood has caused Sergio Garcia many sleepless nights."

Sometimes players' surnames can combine to hilarious effect. John Motson was talking about Ian Cox and Jamie Hand during the Watford v Burnley match when he exclaimed: "The ref has given Burnley a free kick for a foul by Hand on Cox."

An intriguing question from Alan Hansen: "How often have we seen Bergkamp come on his right foot and bend one in?"

TV racing expert Derek Thompson on snowfall, clearly channelling the spirit of Ulrika Jonsson for TalkSport: "I've got nine inches out in front of me."

And Marcus and Darren Bent were a frequent source of amusement when they both played for Ipswich Town FC. As Charlie Nicholas proves with this comment from their match against Bolton Wanderers on *Gillette Soccer Saturday*: "That was a close one for Ipswich, with the Bent lads combining well upfront."

The Antiques Goof Show II

Tim Wonnacott, talking about a musical instrument at Blenheim Palace on *Bargain Hunt,* sounded rather boastful when he informed viewers: "This is the largest organ on display in a private house anywhere in Europe."

Michael Parkinson was probably discussing a drawer in a Georgian chest on *Going For A Song,* when he told Penny Smith: "You will find it quite stiff when you pull it out, and it'll be difficult to get back in."

Bargain Hunt's Tim Wonnacott, talking about an early motorbike klaxon, said: "I'm going to put this down and have a little fiddle around with that magnificent horn."

And here's David Dickinson discussing claims that a pearl inset on an antique mirror allegedly had the power to improve your love life: "I've been rubbing it all morning, and I think it's beginning to work."

Mark Stacey, talking about a German officer's headgear on *Bargain Hunt,* told us: "Such a nice looking helmet really deserves to be shown off."

Angela Rippon, helping a young fella search for valuable items on *Cash In The Attic,* innocently asked: "Would your girlfriend mind if we looked inside her drawers?"

David Barbie, talking about a decorative silver mug to a female contestant on *Bargain Hunt*: "You must handle it, all the pleasure is in handling it." How true . . .

Michael Aspel was referring to an impressive World War I tank when he introduced *Antiques Roadshow* by asking: "How about this for a weapon of iron?" Rather boastful he sounded too . . .

Here's Tim Wonnacott, getting excited about a medieval suit of armour with matching axe on *Bargain Hunt*: "Come and have a look at this chap and his huge chopper!"

Paul Martin, introducing the next item to be auctioned on *Flog It!*: "Let's see what happens when Charlie's helmet goes under the hammer!" I'd rather not.

Confession time on *Bargain Hunt*, as Nigel Hunt discussed door knockers with expert Nigel Smith. "You're a bit of a knockers man," says Hunt. "Yes," replied Smith. "I've come across quite a few in my time."

Eric Knowles was about to give a Chinese screen the once-over on *Going for a Song*, when Anne Robinson revealed: "Eric is going solo with an Oriental piece."

Henry Sandon, discussing porcelain pieces on *Antiques Roadshow*, exclaimed: "Never in my life have I seen a better pair of jugs."

John Laidlaw, describing an antique cane on *Bargain Hunt*, told a lady: "It's easy to handle and a very good length, you frequently see them a lot shorter than this."

And from the same show, here's David Dickinson admiring a busty woman's fine copper pans: "You've got the nicest pair I've seen for a while," he said.

Alistair Appleton, told a startled housewife who was looking for valuables on *Cash in the Attic*: "I can't wait to get in your drawers and have a good rummage."

David Barby, describing the split in the lid of a wooden urn on *Bargain Hunt*: "It looks as though someone's screwed it just a bit too hard."

Here's an extraordinary statement from Tommy Puett: "The 16th-century four-poster bed was originally owned by Mick Jagger and Marianne Faithfull."

A Canadian lady, discussing her fine crockery (of course), told an *Antiques Roadshow* expert: "You recognise my jugs after 20 years but not my face."

David Dickinson, discussing toy cars on *Bargain Hunt*: "Can you imagine the look on a young boy's face when he plays with his Dinky for the first time?"

Cock-Ups and Boobs II

Michaela Strachan was talking about Victorian women riding side-saddle on BBC1's *Countryfile* when she revealed: "Women wore long dresses which made it difficult for them to get a leg over."

Scottish MEP and anti-fur campaigner was talking about fur coats when he told Richard and Judy: "This one is made out of four skins."

Caroline Lucas of the Green Party was discussing the need for urgent change when she told a BBC news reporter: "Believe me, I go to bed every night thinking – what is the most effective way to get action?" Not sure, Caroline, but I reckon Lembit could tell you . . .

Here is some genuine TV listings information for the BBC1 show *Ed & Oucho's Excellent Invention*: "Ed and Oucho try to build the Falconator, an all-terrain vehicle with a custard cannon." (Which is well-known Viz comic slang for an ejaculating penis . . .)

Anna Ryder Richardson, renovating a man's wardrobe on *House Invaders*, told him: "We can even spray your knob gold if you like."

Kevin McCloud, commenting on brickwork for *Grand Designs*: "I was always taught that if you can get your hand inside the crack that was the time to worry . . . it's enormous."

Former *Coronation Street* star Denise Welch was talking about the trap door drop on short-lived ITV game-show Russian Roulette when she revealed: "I'm terrified of going down."

Pop legend Tom Jones was proudly telling Richard Allison about his old hit 'It's Not Unusual' when he bragged: "It was a big one when it first came out in 1965 and it still stands up today."

Andrew Castle was commentating on footage from Elton John's party on *GMTV* when he exclaimed: "Oh look, there's Stephen Gateley, about to go into Joseph."

Veteran news broadcaster Trevor McDonald was trailing an item about a whale on ITN when he said dramatically: "Coming up, Free Willie looking for comfort."

The great spoon-bender Uri Geller was suffering from jungle aches and pains on ITV's *I'm a Celebrity...Get Me Out Of Here*. The following morning, his daughter was talking about a massage on *GMTV* when she said: "I bet he can't wait for Mummy to give him one."

An ex-pupil was discussing a teacher's favourite punishment plimsoll on the nostalgia show *Classmates* when he revealed: "He used to wave it around, it was very floppy. He loved it, thwack across your backside."

Here's Lancastrian antiques expert Paul Hayes talking about collecting figures from children's stories on *Housecall*: "Traditional Pooh will always been very collectable," he said.

Movie legend Susan Sarandon, discussing acting on *Hollywood Greats*: "When it came to sex scenes, no one pulled it off like Burt Lancaster."

Anna Ryder Richardson discussing DIY with a male house-hunter on *House Invaders*: "Okay, show me what you've got 'cos I want to play with it."

Dog wanted Duck to play a game of 'hide the bone' on children's TV show *Dog and Duck*. She replied: "Oh, okay, as long as you don't slip it under the bush like you usually do."

Richard talking to Judy about a food supplement: "The last time I popped it in your mouth, you just swallowed it." But, of course, the longer you stay married, the less it happens . . .

Crufts commentator Frank Kane, talking about a dog: "The Pembroke Corgi belongs to Christine Blance – foxy expression, a lovely bone, captivating in the big ring, she really is a gorgeous bitch."

Linda Lusardi was talking about a carpet she was unrolling to greet her *Come Dine With Me* guests when she said: "Gosh, what a long one; I hope I don't trip over the end."

On *Flog It*, Paul Martin asked a woman why she wanted her husband to stop collecting postcards and get rid of his collection. Mournfully, she replied: "He only gets it out every few years to look at it."

More More More – Sporting Clangers Galore

Willie Thorne, commenting to John Virgo on a positional shot by Jimmy White on *Masters Snooker*: "A couple of inches makes all the difference."

And here's Willie again, talking about long cues to Dennis Taylor at the Powerhouse UK Snooker Semi-Final: "Remember those days when you got your equipment out, wobbling up and down, with a tip on it like a Rowntree's fruit gum?"

Billy Mimms, discussing a Brighton Bears basketball player on *Grandstand*: "We got John Thomas in a great penetration."

Garry Herbert, commentating on rowing: "Andy Hodge stroking the British men and Alex Partridge finishing them off."

Tony Green, talking about Tony O'Shea's missed shots at the excellent Embassy Darts Championship: "Ted Hankey there, taking advantage of O'Shea's misses."

Robert Key, talking about combating Aussie fast bowlers: "You have to make a decision whether to pull McGrath's length."

David Rees-Jones, commentating on the BUPA Indoor

Bowls Championship semi-final between David Gourlay and Noel Kennedy: "Noel could do with another four to six inches and David Gourlay's just changing hands."

A tribute to Arnold Palmer from Peter Alliss: "Arnold – one of golf's great fiddlers, I once saw him take a hacksaw to his shaft and remove three inches from its head just for fun."

Gary Herbert, commentating on the Rowing World Cup: "Britain have managed to get a length up and that'll encourage the Dutch boys to have a sniff."

Here's some expert insight from the great John Motson commentating on Stoke v Man Utd match: "Valencia's very long balls make him quite a handful."

Jessica Holm brought surprising news from Crufts: "Judge Albert Wight has pulled out Willie and that will have Clare Balding jumping with delight."

Ron McIntosh, commentating on wheelchair basketball: "Simon Munn finds Jon Pollock wide open and curls one in the back door."

Let's hope Steve Davies was discussing his drive on C5's Schiehallion Cup golf coverage when he confessed: "I'm struggling in the length department."

Toby Moody, discussing tyres at the Moto GP race on Eurosport: "Andrea Dovizioso has a hard on."

Ashia Hansen, talking about her amazing triple jump at the European Games: "I knew I had a big one in me and was just glad to get it out."

Brandon Riley, commenting on the race position of relay

runners receiving the baton: "Sally Gunnell used to always take it from behind rather than in front."

John Barrett, reporting from Wimbledon: "Kim Clijsters is tinkering down below and finding conditions soggy."

Kelly Holmes, talking about her sprinting finish in the 800m heats: "I just wanted to open my legs because I wasn't sure who was chasing me."

Nigel Starmer-Smith, discussing hockey: "Jane Smith has one of the firmest cracks in women's hockey."

Cricket legend Ian Botham, talking about Andrew Flintoff's bowling: "Andrew uses his length and likes to bang it in."

Virginia Wade, commentating on the Wimbledon ladies doubles final: "Serena puts her hand up very quickly but feels a little stiff and pulls away."

Pam Shriver, discussing Martina Navratilova's munching habits at Wimbledon: "Martina eats so much when the girls change ends."

Here's El Tel on the England v Argentina match: "We've got to squeeze Argentina, otherwise Ortega will come from behind and cause us pain."

Tommy Smythe, commenting on the France v Senegal game: "Camara had a brilliant game, he kept slipping in the back sides of the French players."

Clare Balding, discussing Pat Eddery's riding career on *BBC TV Racing*: "He'll never give up as long as he can get a leg over,"

Derek Thompson, talking about the Haydock race course mascot getting hugged by models on *Channel 4 Racing*: "All the girls love Big Willie."

Bubba Blackwell, yapping away about motorbike stunts on *Extreme Machines*: "You can end up quite sore after a good jump."

Andy Jameson, commentating on the World Swimming Championships: "Popov's got Ian Thorpe behind him, straining to put everything into his back end."

BBC golf commentator Julian Tutt was talking about clubs when he observed: "Ernie Els has the heaviest shaft of anyone on the course."

Sue Barker, chatting to Boris Becker about the advantage of having a powerful serve: "What's it like to have such a big weapon then, Boris?"

Nadia Sawalha was learning to play cricket on Passport To The Sun when she told a Majorcan player: "I'm not very good with balls, I'm surprised you're letting me play with yours."

Sally Gunnell – talking about Jonathan Edwards's triple-jumping ability – declared: "Let's see if Jonathan can pull out a big one. He looks like he could."

Victorious jockey Richard Dunwoody had just won the 2.10 at Hereford when he shared this thought: "I bet Emily Jones on Gajan is thinking 'That's the last time I let Richard up my inner'."

Andrew Raynes, discussing the vertical lift on *The World's Strongest Men*: "It took so much force to get four inches out of the bottom I thought I was going to pass out." Try All-Bran, mate . . .

Alan Shearer was talking about the Fulham v Liverpool match when he remarked: "Duff quickly got round the back of Insua and slipped it in."

Cock-ups And Boobs III

Tracy Shaw, blithering away about water skiing on ITV holiday series *Wish You Were Here* informed us: "If you've got the energy and you like water sports, you can stay wet all day."

Renowned foreign correspondent Matt Frei was talking about the hunt for al-Qaeda fanatics when he told *News at Ten*: "We were taken up the Khyber Pass." Nasty . . .

Richard Bacon, apparently discussing the *Blue Peter* hot air balloon, informed us: "By 6am we were fully erect and raring to go."

Page Three beauty turned broadcaster Dee Evans, talking about showing her future husband Terry Alderton around the house: "I took Terry into my bedroom and showed him my bearskin in front of the fire." Lucky Terry.

Neil Fox, talking about Dani Behr and a contestant's leg injury on ITV's short-lived *Ice Warriors*, said: "If it gets a bit stiff, we'll send Nurse Dani in."

Over on *Whipsnade Zoo*, zoo-keeper John was discussing a pigmy hippo when he said: "She does occasionally go down for a tickle." I've heard the same said about Monica Lewinsky.

The Shopping Channel's top goofer Debbie Flint was discussing a rather naff set of nursery-rhyme figures when she said: "And there's Little Boy Blue, look, he's showing us his little horn."

An embarrassed-looking Beverley Turner, discussing claims that her ex was poorly endowed on *They Think It's All Over,* said: "That was the story in the paper. It did get a bit out of hand." Not *that* small then!

A female vet telling Rolf about an injured cat on *Animal Hospital*: "I've got the noisiest pussy in the country." Thanks for sharing . . .

A lady contestant on *Millionaire* telling Chris Tarrant how she came up with the Christian name of the man behind the Fosbury Flop: "I just opened my mouth and Dick popped out."

Coronation Street star Tracy Shaw, wittering away about being nominated for sexiest soap actress, told *GMTV*: "I'm up for it every year."

Jeremy Bowen, talking about the wind as he hands over the *BBC Breakfast News* weathergirl: "Let's see if she still has it up her."

Clair Frisby, talking about a large hot dog on *Look North*: "There's nothing like a big hot sausage inside you on a cold night like this."

James Lewis, assessing a pitcher on *Bargain Hunt*: "Of course, a pair of jugs is always better than a single one but one is better than none at all."

Russ Williams, talking about a competitor on *Under Pressure*:

"Adrianna embraces her sausage with relish . . . she's straddling the saveloy."

Over on ITV's soft-porn nonsense, *Pleasure Island*, the voiceover woman was talking about a camera when she said: "Boyfriend Barry is always there with his 35 millimetres." Bless!

Here's sound advice from Mag Ruffman, tightening screws on a candle sconce on *Anything I Can Do*: "Make sure you fit the back supports, you'll need them after a lot of screwing."

Nick Owen, talking about his studio Christmas tree: "I hope to get it up this weekend."

Matt Hayes, discussing his complicated angling gear on *Total Fishing*: "No one likes to be accused of having inadequate tackle."

Sadly, Ulrika Jonsson was talking about her weather forecast when she assured morning viewers: "We've just got time for a quick one," adding, "we had it yesterday after the news."

Dishonourable mention – here is a genuine cutting from *Marshwood Vale* magazine, quoted on This Morning: "Visit the Dorset Knob Throwing Festival, besides knob throwing there will be additional fun attractions including knob painting, guess the weight of the big knob, knob darts and a knob pyramid."

Griff Rhys Jones looked fellow canoeist Mary up and down on BBC1's *Rivers* before feeling her jacket with both hands around the chest area and saying: "You're fantastically ell equipped here."

An interesting guide to relaxation from *Come Dine With Me*.

Contestant John was talking about flattening a piece of steak when, he said: "Here's a good way of alleviating stress, beating your meat."

Pause for Sport IX

Willie Carson, talking to Clare Balding about how jockeys prepare to win a big race: "They usually have four or five dreams a night about coming from different positions."

Jim Ross, reporting from the frontline of Sky One's *Wrestlemania*: "Here comes Lita, jerking Edge off . . ."

A Bolex is a make of camera, which is why golf commentator Peter Alliss told the photographer inconsiderately blocking his view: "Move your Bolex to one side, there's a good chap."

Shock revelations from Michael Johnson at the 400 metres: "If Tobin takes it out hard, Malachi Davies is very solid between the legs."

Dave Corkhill, commenting on the bowls: "Paul Foster's trademark is the short jack, splattering everything for 23 metres with his forehand."

Cricket news, as David Lloyd makes this shock announcement during England's first test against the West Indies: "He's pushed his length further up there, has Stuart Broad."

The BBC's Bob Ballard describes Canadian ice hockey player Nick Bender: "Bender taking one off the wrist, he prefers that to the slap."

A shock claim from Paul Dickenson: "Ashia Hansen's spread those legs but the referee has put his red flag up."

Nick Halling, discussing Don Pope on *The World's Strongest Man*: "He's not got much swinging between his legs, relying on his biceps to power it up."

Andy Gray, talking about Paul Warhurst escaping a second yellow card during the Ipswich v Bolton Wanderers game: "Don't get me wrong, I don't like to see players tossed off for nothing . . ."

Julian Tutt, commentating on Tiger Wood at the golf: "Tiger has got the feel and the fingers, but Allenby has the stiffness."

Brendan Foster, commentating on a legendary Ethiopian long-distance runner: "Giving pleasure wherever he goes, Haile Gabrselassie's come out hard. But that won't stop his team-mates trying to pull it off."

Andy Townsend, describing Thierry Henry's possible groin strain: "That would be massive if he had a problem."

Here's Willie Carson talking about jockey Pat Eddery having trouble on his horse during the Irish St Leger: "I'm afraid Pat's in trouble, he's gone down on the Old Man."

David Lloyd, commentating on England's bowling during the second test, made this extraordinary claim: "Jimmy Anderson is swinging both ways this morning."

Trevor Brooking talking about David Beckham's groin strain

during the Germany v England match: "He's certainly led by example this evening, and his injury's stood up superbly."

Paul Dickenson, commentating on Stuart Murray attempting a power-lift on *Britain's Strongest Man*: "He's four inches short but there's his wife Jeannette telling him to hold it back and put his hips forward."

Big Ron Atkinson, commenting on the Man Utd v Bayern Munich game: "Kahn got the flukiest of leg-overs there."

The BBC's Stuart Storey discussing pole-vaulting at the Commonwealth Games: "Nick Buckfield tends to over-shoot when he plants his pole."

And here's Stuart talking about triple-jumper Ashaia Hansen: "Ashaia's a bit ring-rusty, she needs a big one."

Alan Hansen, commenting on the Liverpool v Barcelona match: "Ball in the box, goalkeeper comes all over the place and you know how much I love that."

Cock-Ups And Boobs IV

After comparing heroic real-life copper Ron Caddon to the fictional cops on ITV's *The Bill*, TV-am's Mike Morris told viewers: "We need more Rons to join our police force."

Blockbusters host Bob Holness, asking about a contestant's mascot gift from a pal: "Does your friend always give you one before you appear on TV?"

Michael Aspel put his foot in it during Billy Wright's *This Is Your Life*: "Sadly, Lev Yashin had his leg amputated recently. But it didn't stop him from hopping on a plane to be here tonight."

When talking about infertility on *The Time . . . The Place*, a red-faced lady in the audience protested: "I'm fed up – everyone is having a poke at us."

Paddy McGuinness, trying to decide which celebrity was youngest on BBC2 panel game *Shooting Stars*: "I had to come down the side of Fiona [Bruce]." Dirty boy . . .

An extraordinary revelation from BBC newsreader Sophie Raworth: "John Sergeant's routines left him with bottom marks three weeks in a row." Must be the tight trousers . . .

Over on *Pebble Mill*, Judy Spiers was interviewing a wine expert about his experiences on a nudist beach: "Now tell the audience what popped up," she said.

Here's a strange boast from Tess Daly on *Strictly Come Dancing*: "Everyone is welcome in my backstage area." Go on, Brucie, higher, higher . . .

Jake Robinson, discussing DIY on BBC1's *Big Strong Boys*, told the startled home owner: "Put your knee there, and your hand there, and I'll screw from the other side."

A nun telling the *Two Fat Ladies* about how she looks after her herd of cattle: "I have a man every week," she said.

Carenza Lewis, discussing hunting for food in the Middle Ages on *Time Team Live*: "You could eat beaver if you could get it."

Edward Kennedy, talking about his nephew William who was facing a rape trial, told US news reporters: "I don't believe it – all the family love Willie."

Mariella Frostrup, discussing a helicopter pilot on *Video View*, said: "He's ever so good at handling his chopper."

US wrestling commentator Gorilla Monsoon, talking about the engagement ring WWF star Macho Man had bought the lovely Miss Elizabeth: "He's building up his confidence, he's reaching for it, he's getting it out . . ."

Big Jack Charlton, talking about taking a shot at goal: "Giannini should have shot himself."

A guest hairdresser discussing hairstyles on *This Morning*: "All brides like a bit of body before they get married."

Tom O'Connor the host of ITV quiz-show *Crosswits*, was talking to Dinah Sheridan about previous editions, when he said: "It seems like only yesterday that we were on the game together."

Timmy Mallet should really get a grip on himself; when star guest Kylie Minogue got a wrong answer in his mallet quiz on *Wacaday*, tiresome Timmy told her: "I think you deserve a bonk for that."

John Sessions, discussing his limitations as a mimic, confessed: "I really don't have what it takes to do Liz Taylor."

TV-am's Richard Keys was talking about retrieving lost hamsters when a female caller came on with this useful advice: "Just shake your nuts under the floorboards and they'll come running."

Strange question from Des Lynam to Christine Truman: "How do you feel about the men's tackle this year?" Thankfully, he was talking about male tennis fashions.

Miriam Stoppard was hosting a discussion on the new X-rated satellite Adult Channel on *People Today*. Just as a clip of a couple getting passionate was flashed up on the screen, Miriam rather alarmingly asked: "How big do you think it will get?"

Here's bird-brained *Top of the Pops* presenter Anthea Turner, talking about Cher's long stay at Number One: "Nobody's been able to knock her off," she assured us.

Handyman Doug Smillie was putting up shelves on *Bazaar* when he startled Nerys Hughes by smiling and telling her: "We're ready for screwing now."

TV-am's Mike Morris was discussing White House interest in astrology: "Ronald Reagan? Oh yes, he's an aquarium." And to think some cruel bearded TV critic nicknamed Mike 'The Plank'...

Back when she was a stunning weathergirl, Ulrika Jonsson was actually discussing the new 5p coin when she came out with this mind-boggling statement: "I was playing with it for ages, but I found it was too small. It kept slipping through my fingers. I prefer a big one." So, nothing changes then . . .

Here's Jonathon Pearce commentating on BBC1's naff celebrity game-show *Hole In The Wall*: "Sophie Anderton has no trouble bending herself into all the right places while John contorts himself into position behind her."

Bruno Tonioli was talking about dancing technique on *Strictly Come Dancing* when he told the great Welsh boxer Joe Calzaghe what to with his dance partner Kristina Rihanoff: "Get down on her, use her, make the most of what she's got... play with it." But would Kristina have minded if he'd misunderstood? I was more perturbed when Alesha congratulated Rav Wilding for "giving it your hole."

Pause For Sport X

The new stand at Doncaster race course took Brough Scott's breath away. "My word," he said, "Look at that magnificent erection."

During a tense snooker match, commentator Jack Karnehm remarked: "This is a very difficult shot as there's just 1½ inches between the balls."

A shock revelation from Andy Townsend: "It's a nightmare when you've got Arshavin in the hole."

Reg Gutteridge, talking about boxer Mike Weaver: "He might be a bit slow on his legs, but he can still bang a bit."

Howzat for a howler! Jack Bannister bowled a googly when he remarked: "The Australians really fancy Graham Gooch around the short-leg area."

Snooker commentator Clive Everton was talking about Steve James' use of a cue rest: "His tackle is coming out to its full length," he said

Cricketer Richie Richardson shot up in pain after being struck in the wedding tackle during a vital Test match. Richie Benaud was commentating on the over: "That's two balls gone

– Lewis to continue bowling." Ouch!

Paul Dickenson was talking about a high-jump competitor at the World Athletics when he claimed: "50,000 people will be hoping for a German, Spank, on Friday night."

Greg Harlow, commentating at the World Bowls contest: "Mervyn King, Jack's off and the markers will be praying they don't have to measure his length."

Mike Atherton was probably after bowling tips from England cricketer Jimmy Anderson when he asked him: "What's more important the wrist position or the feelings in the fingers?"

Jim Rosenthal, talking about Peter Beardsley's soccer technique: "Beardsley is now on top and working hard to get it in."

Brian Moore, talking about Pierre Littbarski's throw-in during the West Germany v Italy football match: "For a little man it's really quite a long one."

Goof, set and match to tennis commentator Dan Maskell for this howler: "Lendl returned that well, but created an enormous hole for himself down his back side."

Stewart Storey's verdict on Dawn Harper's 2009 100m hurdles victory: "She had the wind behind her and the others never got a sniff."

Ian 'Beefy' Botham, discussing pre-match rituals on Sky Sport 2: "I always liked a quick run to get rid of the stiffness." I never doubted it . . .

Mark James, talking about how cold links golf courses can be: "I remember Ken Brown used to soak his balls in hot water for

30 minutes before going out to play."

Chris Baillieu talking about the Oxford-Cambridge Boat Race: "Greasing their seats and putting everything in will leave these two crews with very sore backsides."

Ron Atkinson: "I never criticise referees and I'm not going to change a habit for that prat."

David Coleman on Linford Christie's finishing power during the Tokyo World Championships: "He's got a habit of pulling it out when it matters."

Dave Corkill, commenting on *Indoor Bowls*: "Debbie Stavrou has been favouring a longer length all week."

Steve Ryder, covering the US Masters golf: "Ballesteros felt much better today after a 69." I'm not at all surprised . . .

Michael Slater, anticipating a West Indies declaration on *Test Match Cricket*: "England players are waiting to see Jimmy Adams' hand pulling his batsmen off."

Ken Brown, talking about Nick Faldo's caddie Fanny Sunneson at the Open: "Condition's saturated, so Fanny will have to keep the muscles moving."

Gourmet Gaffes II – More Cooking Cock-Ups

Telly chef Jamie Oliver, talking about whipping eggs: "I have to go through the pain barrier till it's nice and stiff, but you can be quite rough with it."

Chef Albert Roux, was discussing the quality of the cooking on BBC4's trouble-shootings series *Trouble At The Top*, when he revealed: "Bill gave me a sample of his sausage. It was fantastically succulent."

TV chef Glyn Christian said of a large royal show bull and its equally huge lady owner: "Just look at the size of this beast. I don't think I've ever seen one as big. Oh! I mean the bull!" Well recovered, sir.

Gordon Ramsay, was discussing Chinese noodles, I expect, when he announced: "A minimum of six pulls is required to get the right thickness." Although I've heard Japanese bath house girls say much the same thing...

And here's crinkle-faced chef Gordon talking about a salad on Cookalong Live: "You have to toss it just right to get that zingy taste in your mouth."

Little Ronnie Corbett was peeling orange zest on *Open House*, when he asked Anne Stirk: "How much do you want me to put in?" "As much as you can manage," she replied. Tsk. As brazen as you like . . .

Bazaar chef Lesley Waters was talking about baking beef cobblers when she instructed viewers: "First you must get your cobblers and brush them with milk."

John Burton-Race broke in to a crème brulee with a spoon on ITV's *Britain's Best Dish*. As the hard surface split in two, Mark Nichols turned to him and said "Wow, look at that crack."

Celebrity MasterChef voice-over, talking about contender *Holby City* star Mark Moraghan: "Before Mark starts cooking he has to bone the rabbit." Blimey. That's a bit strong for BBC1.

Michael O'Keefe was speculating about how fellow contestant, Bruce Mainwearing would perform on **Come Dine With Me** when he said, "I think he's going to pull it off tonight." That's what I call a climax to a meal

Foot in Mouth V

Big Ron Atkinson: "I'm going to make a prediction – it could go either way." You don't say, Ron.

David Platt: "Craig Bellamy's got pace, but he's also rapid as well."

Paul Merson: "I don't think Arsenal will finish above Arsenal." Although it'd be a good trick to pull off if they could.

Tyrone James: "When you play football, two things happen – the wife can't get to you, the bank manager can't get to you and you have no responsibility."

Lawrie McMenemy: "The last person to score a hat-trick in a final was Stan Mortenson. He had a final named after him – the Matthews Final."

Harry Carpenter on heavyweight boxer Gary Mason: "Oh, what a good left hook – and Mason can throw them with either hand!"

Sean Rafferty: "He was a wonderful man, as was his wife."

Roger Federer: "In tennis there has to be a winner sometimes."

Classic clanger from Richie Benaud: "That slow-motion replay doesn't show how fast the ball was travelling."

Ron Pickering on a London Marathon runner: "He's letting his legs do the running."

Tony Adams: "Arshavin is a great player; the kid can play. And best of all, he's not a kid."

Brian Johnston: "Turner looks a bit shaky and unsteady, but I think he's going to bat on - one ball left."

David Turner: "Kenny Miller will make his second debut."

Peter Willey: "Flintoff can only play one way and that's 110 per cent. Every ball he bowls is 100 per cent."

Emile Heskey: "You can never say never. Unless you say never yourself."

Phil Brown: "Manachu had three shots. Two of them were wild, one was better and the fourth was decisive."

Malcolm Allison: "Size does matter in football. You judge a defender by the size of his tackle."

Ron Atkinson: "It's all about the two 'M's – movement and positioning."

Cock-ups And Boobs V

Kathy Burke was talking about a mathematical challenge on *Room 101* when she told Paul Merton: "I couldn't handle a big eight."

Former Spice Girl star Emma Bunton was chatting away about kissing on her VH1 show when she said: "I want to see everyone out there snogging. Anyone without a partner just use your hand."

Here's a surprise confession from Laurence Llewelyn-Bowen on *Home Front*: "To find out what the houses were like before, I've knocked up a couple of neighbours."

Anna Richards, discussing a Dick Turpin film on *Time Tales*: "I can't resist one last look at Dick, for old times' sake." Few women can...

Here's Miranda Schunker's bird-watch update on GMTV: "We've seen a few tits this morning." Yeah, and none bigger than Richard Arnold.

Fred Dibnah, talking about melting lead for the roof of St Paul's Cathedral on *Magnificent Monuments*: "Imagine a young lad, with a pig's bladder, you know, furiously pumping away."

Katy Knapman, describing a gold identity bracelet on the Shop! Channel: "This is nine inches in length, which is the perfect size for any man."

Richard Hammond, commenting on BBC1's *Total Wipe-Out* contender Sarah, a white witch: "She might well do something magic with those big balls."

Michaela Strachan, having been chased by geese on *The Really Wild Show* announced: "Now I've been thoroughly goosed."

Jason Gardiner was discussing skating with Coleen Nolan on ITV's Dancing On Ice when he told her: "What you lack in technique you make up for with your performance . . . do you feel he has a stiffer core now?" Easy, fella . . .

Robert Kilroy-Silk, discussing embarrassing moments on his BBC1 morning series *Kilroy*: "What about the chap who dropped his trousers on the show? I just had to handle it."

Ulrika Jonsson was talking about rainfall on TVam when she assured viewers: "I just can't get enough of it" – although, frankly, no one would have been surprised if she'd meant cock.

Steve Leonard was talking about vegetation on *Vets in the Wild* when he asked delightful Norweigan vet Trude Mostue: "When did you last Hoover in this dining room? There's something big growing between my legs."

Penny Smith, talking about the 'obey' in the wedding service on *GMTV*: "I wanted it left out, but the vicar just slipped it in."

This is from the Channel 4 programme guide: "*The Perfect Penis*, a look at how the search for a bigger longer penis has driven men to extraordinary lengths."

Dishonourable mention – genuine newspaper headline, quoted on Have I Got News For You: 'Minister resigns over Brown smears'.

Mark Stacey was describing some metal statuettes of firemen on *Flog It!* when he remarked: "Unfortunately, one of the firemen has lost the end off of his chopper."

Contestant Natalie was talking about an allegedly lucky quartz stone she'd been given on *Come Dine With Me when she complained:* "I've been rubbing it but I've been told I've got to rub it some more, 'cos nothing's happening."

Dawn of the Dumb

One of the small joys of television is the stupid questions given by contestants on quiz shows. Here are ten of my all-time favourites:

University Challenge. Bamber Gascoigne asked what Ghandi's first name was. The contestant replied "Goosey?"

National Lottery In It To Win It. Dale Winton asked the player to name the world's largest continent. He replied: "The Pacific."

University Challenge. Jeremy Paxman asked: "What is another name for cherry-pickers and cheesemongers?" The answer was regiments in the British Army. The contestant answered: "Homosexuals."

BBC1's Dog Eat Dog, Ulrika Jonsson wanted to know who wrote the Lord of the Rings. The contestant answered "Enid Blyton."

ITV's The Vault. Melanie Sykes asked: "What is the name given to the condition where the sufferer can fall asleep at any time?" The answer was narcolepsy. The woman playing replied: "Nostalgia."

The Weakest Link. Anne Robinson asked "In traffic, what is

the 'j' where two roads meet. The contestant replied "Jewel carriageway."

The National Lottery. Eamonn Holmes asked: "Dizzy Gillespie is famous for playing what?" The contestant was sure of the answer. "Basketball," he replied.

Anne Robinson was looking for the answer Jar Jar Banks on The Weakest Link when she asked "What fictional character in Star Wars beginning 'Jar Jar' was named as the most irritating film character of all time?" The contestant replied: "Zsa Zsa Gabor."

On Fifteen-To-One, William G. Stewart asked: "Above the entrance to which place do the words "Abandon all hope, ye who enter here" appear?" The contestant replied "A Church." The answer was Hell.

ITV's The Vault. Melanie Sykes asked: "In which European city was the first opera house opened in 1637?" The contestant answered: "Sydney."

Pause For Sport XI

Golf coach Butch Harmon was demonstrating how to take a shot on Sky Sports when he said: "You need a little cock in your left wrist."

Back when she was Gaby Yorath, Gaby Logan was talking about the Premiership relegation dog-fight when she remakred: "Let's have a look at the bottom and see just how tight it is down there."

Jamie Redknapp, commentating on the World Cup: "If he plays, Michael Owen and Wayne Rooney will have it off against Marcel Desailly."

Here's Steve Cram covering the BBC World Athletics Championship, 2009: "Usain Bolt opens his legs and we all draw breath, the big man always rises to the occasion."

Pole-vault champ Kate Dennison was talking about improving her vaults when she assured us: "I just need to get a grip and the big ones will soon come."

Peter Drury, commentating on the Boat Race: "Cambridge cox waiting for the first stroke . . . just as soon as Rebecca Dowbiggin's hand comes down."

Howard Clark, talking about the rough at the Ryder Cup: "It's seven inches long and growing."

Willie Thorne commentating on China's snooker ace Ding Junhul: "He's got a chink in his armour." Who writes his script, Anton Du Beke?

Here's how the Eurosport commentator decribed the end of the Men's 800 metre final at the 2008 World Junior Championships in Poland: "Kaki from Sudan wins it, with Kibet of Kenya second. Followed by the South African Olivier with the Pole in his rear."

Jason Goodall, painting an amazing picture of Amelie Mauresmo's sterling performance at Wimbledon: "She gave the groin a good workout and spent two sets putting her forehand in Cervanova's box."

Gary Herbert, reporting from World Cup Rowing: "Britain's women are enjoying this – a good length up and giving it a bit of push."

Tony Gubba, commentating on the Bradford v Watford game on *Match of the Day*: "The goalie was injured as Robinson followed through."

Show-jumping authority Mike Tucker, talking about a horse of course: "Ollie Townsend's riding Tom Cruise, who's supple and loose but he's had nine other jockeys."

Eurosport's David Goldstrum, reporting from the World Weightlifting Championships: "These Saudi Arabians have the wobbliest snatches I've ever seen. And at 140 kilos you don't want one of them coming down on your head."

A stunning revelation from Clive Tyldersley at Euro 2004: "Marian Pahars is imminent...He's stripped off and ready to come."

Willie Carson, commentating on the Queen Elizabeth II horse race: "Frankie Dettori looking down between his legs and all he can see is Peslier up his backside."

German ski-jumper Andreas Wank is still making life difficult for Eurosport commentator David Goldstrum, who informed viewers: "Manuel Fettner is airborne, he's got a metre and a half in his hand. Wank's live on German TV."

Just a few days earlier, Goldstrum kept a remarkably straight face when he said: "Werner Schuster of Germany will be eagerly watching Andreas Wank, but he'll be disappointed with the 119 metres he managed."

Peter Beagrie was describing an Arsenal goal against Sheffield United on *Gillette Soccer Special* when he said: "Merida turned with two men up his backside..." adding in the same sentence, "These guys play with a smile on their faces."

And the Goofs Go On

Charlie Dimmock was helping Alan Titchmarsh with a tree stake on *Ground Force*. "How far in am I?" he asked. "About eight inches." Charlie replied, breathlessly. "But it needs a few more inches."

Fiona Phillips stunned GMTV viewers by announcing: "It's live, it's large and it's going up today." Mercifully, she was talking about the Millennium Wheel.

A vet on *Daytime Live* told Floella Benjamin: "If tortoises don't eat enough in the summer, when they hibernate they wake up dead."

Mike Smith asked a mum on *No Kidding*: "I hear you've been to see the Chippendales – did anything about them stick out in particular?"

Rob Curling on the BBC news: "A police officer from Kent will appear in court tomorrow on a charge of supplying cannabis after a joint investigation."

Roy Walker to an understandably nervous contestant on *Catchphrase*: "We're putting the money up, you're behind."

Nick Brooks-Ward reported excitedly from the 2009 *Horse Of*

The Year Show on the BBC. "Peter Charles," he said. "So much power between his legs, working it with his hands in front of Olivia Newton-John and Susan George who are enjoying hospitality." I've never heard it called that before...

Richard Madeley to Julian Lennon on *This Morning*: "Do you think you owe your success to what's in your genes?"

Winner turned judge Alesha Dixon was talking about Phil Tufnell's dance posture on BBC1's *Strictly Come Dancing* when she told him: "You can't keep relying on your buttocks, as much as we like a bit of bum action..."

Over on Project Catwalk, one of the models was talking about a designer and her fashions when she said: "We get on well and I think I pull off her clothes well too."

Classic Coleman Clangers

A Tribute to the Original Guvnor of the Goof – the Top Ten of David Coleman cock-ups

"For those watching who haven't got television sets, the live commentary is on Radio Two."

"That's the fastest time ever run – but it's not as fast as the world record."

"This man could be a black horse."

"The late start is due to the time."

"And there go the two leaders – Boutayeb, Aouita and Baccouche."

"She's not Ben Johnson, but then who is?"

"He is even smaller in real life than he is on the track."

"We estimate, and this isn't an estimation, that Greta Waltz is 80 seconds behind."

"This race is all about racing."

"The news from the javelin is that it was won by that winning throw we saw earlier."

And let's not forget Murray Walker. Here are five of his finest sayings:

"With half the race gone, there's half the race still to go!"

"Prost can see Mansell in his earphones."

"Two laps to go and then the action will begin. Unless this is the action, which it is."

"The young Ralf Schumacher has been upstaged by teenager Jenson Button, who is 20."

"And now the boot is on the other Schumacher." Eh?

Pause For Sport XII

Andy Gray, discussing a Man Utd v Arsenal match on Sky Sports, informed us: "He's got a soft one, so Sol Campbell won't be happy with Wayne Rooney going down on him so easily." Indeed . . .

Chris Snode, commentating on women's diving pairs at the 2008 Summer Olympics: "Ukrainian girls with their legs open . . . judges take a look, a lot of diving has gone on there."

Nick Mullins, raising eyebrows while commentating on the rugby EDF Energy Cup: "Andy Farrell hands on De Kock and he's making it available for Leonelli to play with."

Here's a startling revelation from Colin Bryce at the Women's luge: "Anke Wischnewski, flat on her back, going at 111 kilometers an hour, powered only by her flaps."

And a classic from race commentator Ted Walsh: "This is really a lovely horse
and I speak from experience since I once mounted her mother."

A shock admission from Chicago Bears star Jim McMahon: "Sometimes I feel so good my balls start to spiral."

Match Of The Day's Steve Wilson was talking about a Wigan Athletic footballer's change of direction and not of his sexuality when he blurted out the shock statement: "Emile Heskey's already on the turn."

Here's a surprising verdict from US tennis ace turned commentator Tracy Austin at Wimbledon: "Sharapova's tossing hasn't been that good." Tsk. Everyone's a critic.

An amazing prediction from Olympics boxing commentator Jim Neilly: "The big Cuban's going to come like a steam train."

Here's boxing trainer Freddie Roach boasting about his boy's big right hand...I hope: "Amir Khan has a great tool."

Former world welterweight champ Ricky Hatton was talking about nothing ruder than watching a bout when he told a sports repoerter: "Muhammad Ali's daughter Laila is a very fit girl. I'd like to see her box." Wouldn't we all?

Here's Charlie Nicholas commentating on a busy Arsenal mid-fielder running rings round the opposition: "Jack Wilshere has completely sucked two centre-backs."

BBC boxing commentator Ritchie Woodhall was talking about body punches in an Olympic boxing bout when he observed: "The Thai champ doesn't like it inside him." The Pink Pounder on the other hand...

Here's a very reasonable thought from Spurs mid-fielder David Bentley: "I hope the manager doesn't come in my car."

Not quite a goof but it made my ears prick up when the BBC commentator said of Lewis Hamilton's prang at Monza: "He crashed between two Lesmos."

Alan Shearer commenting on the footballing action as Cardiff City played Portsmouth when he said: "Paul Parry is pulling off Sol Campbell time and time again."

Indian cricket ace Anil Kumble was talking about his remarkable spin-bowling when he commented: "Ten inches is quite a lot when it's as hard as that." I'll say it is.

Arsenal manager Arsene Wenger discussing Theo Walcott's style of playing: "Sometimes he can be an 'in and out' player, but when he's in he's completely in."

A surprising insight from Dutch footballer Bolo Zenden discussing his manager's ability to relate to his team: "Guus Hiddink knows how to touch players."

French football ace Antoine Sibierski was in a hands-on mood after winning a match when he told a TV sports reporter: "I was happy because when you touch many balls, you enjoy. And I enjoyed."

Here's Spanish football manager Rafa Benitez talking about getting inside information: "I always enjoy it internally."

The ever reliable David Goldstrum was commenting on Canadian sculling partners Melanie Kok and Tracy Cameron for Eurosport when he revealed: "Cameron is stroking, Kok in the bow seat, and very experienced at is she is as well."

Ann Jones, commenting on the 1987 Ladies Doubles final at Wimbledon: "How much better a doubles match is when all four players are alive."

An eye-brow raising revelation from Paul Merson: "To be a top manager, you have to be a bit the other way."

Here's BBC Sport's Matt Chilton commentating on the World Rowing Championships: "Long, powerful Eric Murray is stroking the New Zealanders' semi."

Sky Sports Ian Darke was talking about a shot on goal when he sighed: "Beckford, looking for one of those benders but they haven't come off tonight."

Here's David Pleat discussing Spain's footballing performance: "Sergio Ramos doesn't look too happy as he pumps away."

Greg Rusedski was talking about tennis when he goofed: "Both players are getting a good feel of the balls."

Brighton & Hove Albion footballer Adam Virgo was discussing his plans for the match against Man City when he announced: "I intend to get on top of Robinho as quickly as possible."

Commentator Robin Jackman on cricket ace Ian Botham: "There's nothing Botham likes better than a maiden or two under his belt."

Here's Steve Wilson talking about pre-penalty tension when he appeared to spot some Monica Lewinsky style behaviour on the terraces: "There were a few thousand people behind that goal sucking like mad."

This is BBC Sport's Arlo White commentating on a cricket match that sounded like it should have been screened by TVX: The Fantasy Channel: "And Pietersen's just stroked Vettori through the covers."

A surprising revelation from Fernando Torres talking about

Rafa Benitez's attitude to the Anfield changing room: "I know that Rafa has tried to get it extended several times."

Over on Match Of The Day Gus Poyet was asked what he thought of Spurs languishing at the foot of the Premier League. "Who likes being stuck in the bottom?" he shrugged. Well, aside from Justin Fashanu, that is.

ITV's Jim Beglin sounded like he was auditioning for a Clearasil advert when he discussed a header during the England v Croatia football match: "Johnson thought Eduardo was just going to pick a spot on his head."

On Sky Sports, cricket pundit Allan Donald was referring to South Africa's opening bowler Andrew Nel when he observed: "It must take it out of you, banging it in all day like that."

ITV Sport's Gabriel Clarke was talking about the pitch when he told viewers: "I'm assured it's the best Dutch grass money can buy."

A BBC newsreader was talking about the 2010 World Cup when she said: "England's finals base will be in Phoeking, South Africa." Not that bad is it?

The other drivers breathed a collective sigh of relief when Formula One world champion Lewis Hamilton promised: "I'm not planning on going up the inside of anyone."

Here he is apparently boasting: "I come here with a strong feeling and a good package."

And here's Lewis again talking cobblers: "It's about the driver with the biggest balls who can get closest to the barriers."

Foot In Mouth VI

Justin Langer: "Cricket looks an easy game when you're listening to it on the radio."

Chris Kamara: "Jimmy Bullard had two free kicks. He scored one, nearly scored from one and missed one."

David Pleat: "Andorra will literally park the bus in front of the goal."

Steve Tilson: "Southend and Doncaster are the league's top scorers so it was always going to be 0-0."

Sven-Goran Eriksson: "Everyone knows what happens now, but nobody knows."

Dean Kiely: "There's nothing between these two sides, but Birmingham have had the better of it."

Graeme Souness: "At the Euros, Ibrahimovich never touched the ball, although I know he scored."

Phil Thompson: "For Man City to go from where they are to where they are is too much to expect."

Kevin Pietersen: "It's really good to see Michael with his head back on."

Joe Calzaghe: "If you want to be a boxer you can't fight for money, although I fight for money."

Roy Keane: "Sometimes, you've got to lose to win."

Kevin Blackwell: "Schwarzer made a great save, although I don't think he got a touch on it."

Sepp Blatter: "Before the problem was tackling from behind, but now the players are doing it from the front and the side; this is a matter we'll discuss." (yes because the correct way to tackle is to swoop down from the skies).

Mark Lawrenson: "This is Spain playing but it isn't Spain."

Serena Williams: "I'm currently writing a screenplay that I haven't started yet."

Charlie Nicholas: "To win this game, Celtic will have to score a goal."

Chris Kamara: "The lad's only kicked out at the defender's back and that can't be violent conduct."

John Motson: "Thierry Henry I fancy!"

Gary Newbon: "There'll be more football in a moment, but first we've got highlights of the Scottish Cup Final."

Avram Grant: "Arsenal didn't have one single chance, including the goal."

Aldershot's Gary Waddock: "I'm pleased for our fans and also our supporters."

TV commentator at Goodwood: "There's a jockey down there walking around on his feet."

Glen Hoddle: "If United win 2-0 and Saha scores both, at the end of the day he'll have two goals."

Jim Beglin: "Exactly the same thing happened with Alexander Frei. Although it was a different injury."

Tony Lewis, commentating during the 1987 Pakistan-England cricket Test, said: "That's how it looked in slow motion, but it went a lot quicker than that."

World Gymnastics Championship commentator: "He is what Nadia Komanee and Olga Korbut were to men's' gymnastics."

Graeme Souness: "It's the big players who make the decisions at half-time. Although not the decisions."

Phil Thompson: "Under Juande Ramos, the Spurs players didn't have any legs."

Ex-Spurs boss David Pleat became a king of cock-ups. Here are three of his greatest gaffes:

"We just ran out of legs."

"Had we not got that second goal, I think the score might have been different. But I'm not sure."

"Winning is not the end of the world."

They Called It What?

Okay, I know these aren't TV goofs but I thought these genuine shop and place names from around the world would tickle you as much as they tickled me....

Parisian hotel name: Hotel Kuntz

A supermarket in Turkey: UFUK Market

A cafe in San Fransisco: Squat & Gobble

Chinese restaurant in Sheffield: Mange

A petrol station in Bavaria: Wank Garage

Fishing shop in Florida: Master Bait & Tackle

From a menu in Zante, Greece: Aborigines with cheese in the oven.

Sign in an Orlando bar: Wine your Valentine. Liquor too.

Devon farm name: Prickly Ball Farm.

Australian street: Bald Knob Road

Lincoln street: The Glory Hole

Skegness street: Fanny Hands Lane

Sheffield steet: Butt Hole Road (that sounds like a dump)

Paris street: Rue De Bitche

Northampton street: The Knob.

Street in Wolverhampton: Hardon Road

Street sign in China: No Chewing Cum

Ukrainian burger bar: MkWenk

Cab firm in Poland: Taxi Fart

Hotel in Dortmund: Hotel Bender

Polish shop name: fuks33

Australian town: Wankerville

Irish town: Muff

English village: Cockadilly

Irish town: Gaggin

Worcestershire village: Bell End

Austrian town: Fucking

Spanish village: Tossa

Cumbrian village: Slaggyford

Manchester district: Nob End

Restaurant in Bonn: Muckefuck

Budapest restaurant: Fatal

Museum in Tallinn, Estonia: "Kiek in de Kok."

German sausage brand: Knacker Rote Wurst

An unfortunate abbreviation of assorted fudge spotted in a

York shop: Ass Fudge

Pause For Sport XIII

Tanya Stevenson was talking about the going at Haydock Park when she said to jockey Kieren Fallen: "Obviously it is pretty soft out there, softer than you were expecting, but you handled it better with faster conditions."

Ross King, discussing relays with champion runner Phil Redmond, asked: "Well Phil, tell us about your amazing third leg."

Winston Bennett, University of Kentucky basketball forward: "I've never had major knee surgery on any other part of my body."

Here's heavyweight boxing champ Lennox Lewis on his beaten opponent Mike Weaver: "I took my time until he exposed himself, and then I let him have it."

TV commentator during the mixed marathon: "Many of the female contestants are getting nearer the front and starting to break wind."

Darts ace Jocky Wilson scored 180, prompting commentator Sid Waddell to exclaim: "Oh, what a time to pull it out!"

BBC newscaster Debbie Hall tickled *Breakfast Time* viewers

when she announced: "Horse trainer Fred Winter is in hospital in a stable condition."

During a dispute about distances in the 1987 CIS Bowls championship, the ref hollered at a startled assistant: "One inch, Willie." Poor Willie.

During the 1990 World Cup, Barry Davies said of one of the Holland team: "I wonder how he feels, his first game in a Dutch cap."

Here's Jimmy Greaves talking about the Northampton V Southampton match on Saint and Greavsie: "It will be the biggest Hampton that wins."

Classic cock-up from Guy Michelmore: "Many supporters say they wouldn't stand for all-seater stadiums."

Leon Wood, New Jersey Nets guard, to Steve Albert, Nets TV commentator: "Are you any relation to your brother Marv?"

And here's the legendary US baseball pitcher Jerome 'Dizzy' Dean, explaining how he felt after being hit on the head by a ball in the World Series: "The doctors X-rayed my head and found nothing."

The Lunatics Have Taken Over The Asylum

Politicians may regard themselves as a cut above the general herd, but they are not above mangling their words spectacularly. Here are some of the all-time great political goofs

George W. Bush was the king of the cock-up of course. He once told the good people of Nashua, New Hampshire: "I know how hard it is for you to put food on your family."

Bush referred to "peacekeeper" as "pacemaker" and argued that America "cannot let terrorists and rogue nations hold this nation hostile" rather than "hostage."

In South Carolina, he got philosophical with supporters: "Rarely is the question asked, Is our children learning?" he said.

Debating with John McCain, Bush made this point: "I think we agree, the past is over."

Geo's greatest goofs include "Families is where our nation finds hope, where wings take dream." And "I know the human being and fish can coexist peacefully."

But this has to be my all-time favourite: "Our enemies are innovative and resourceful, and so are we. They never stop thinking about new ways to harm our country and our people, and neither do we."

But his Democratic challenger Al Gore was little better, coming out with corkers like: "A zebra doesn't change its spots."

In the US, Bush's only serious cock-up competitor was the senator Dan Quayle whose bloopers included:

"It isn't pollution that's harming the environment. It's the impurities in our air and water that are doing it."

"I believe we are on an irreversible trend toward more freedom and democracy - but that could change."

"The Holocaust was an obscene period in our nation's history. I mean in this century's history. But we all lived in this century. I didn't live in this century."

"What a waste it is to lose one's mind. Or not to have a mind is being very wasteful. How true that is."

"Republicans understand the importance of bondage between a mother and child."

"Unfortunately, the people of Louisiana are not racists."

Other classic political howlers include:

"I haven't committed a crime. What I did was fail to comply with the law." - David Dinkins, New York City Mayor, answering accusations that he failed to pay his taxes.

"Smoking kills. If you're killed, you've lost a very important part of your life." – Brooke Shield, during an interview to become spokesperson for a federal anti-smoking campaign.

"Outside of the killings, Washington has one of the lowest crime rates in the country." Mayor Marion Barry, Washington, DC

"The streets are safe in Philadelphia. It's only the people who make them unsafe." Frank Rizzo, ex-police chief and mayor of Philadelphia.

Cock-ups And Boobs VI

A shock confession from gay Richard Arnold on *GMTV*: "The first things I paid for with a credit card were three 12-inchers." He was talking about vinyl singles. Probably.

On BBC1's *Churchill* series, Winston's former secretary was reflecting on how the great man constructed his speeches, informing us: "He tried and tried all night long, but he just could not make it come." Wonder if Paddy Pants-down ever had the same problem...

Richard Park was talking about Ewan McGregor's skill with the French horn on *Greatest TV Wannabe Moments* when he goofed: "He's fantastic at everything he does and I think that probably just about includes the horn."

Celebrity contestant Tim Rice came up with the word 'panties' on *Countdown*. Richard Whiteley turned to Carol Vorderman and sternly told her: "Let's have panties down, Carol."

Tim Wonnacott was discussing a pair of silver sugar tongs made in the shape of a wishbone and discovered by expert Catherine Southon on *Bargain Hunt* when he said: "Let's go across to the auctioneer and see what he thinks of Catherine's novelty nips."

Continuity announcer on ITV's *Britain's Best Dish*: "Coming up, Jilly opens up and there's a split over the starters."

Jane Garvey was talking about the *Miss World* contest being televised by Sky One when she said: "I hope my husband will be entering me."

Douglas Hurd raised a few eyebrows on BBC1's *Question Time* when he revealed: "I spent most of the day on a boat on the Thames going up and down with the ladies."

Here's a right regal ricket from Tom Fleming, commentating on the Queen's 1988 birthday parade: "You can see the Queen's carriage and the colonel's behind."

TVam viewers were taken aback when Ulrika Jonsson confided: "I'm having problems with boyfriend withdrawal."

A fella who had taken his teddy bear all around the world told viewers of *The Time…The Place*: "This bear has circumcised the entire world."

Commenting on a procession of different food on *Daytime Live*, Judi Spiers remarked: "And now, bringing up the rear, we have prunes."

Richard Whiteley stunned contestants on *Countdown* when he asked them: "Well, who wants to have a go with Carol?"

Chef Jill Myers was talking about ways of making a chocolate pudding on *Farmhouse Kitchen* when she said: "You can do it this way, but I've actually made this one sitting on the pan." Let's hope she washed her hands.

Dietician Patrick Holford was discussing the oil content of food on Rosemary Conley's *Diet And Fitness* programme when he said "If you set fire to your nuts, you'll soon discover how much oil they contain."

Classic Clanger – a *Blockbusters* contestant to Bob Holness: "I fancy a P now, please Bob."

Attractive classical violinist Nicola Benedetti was rightly praised for her brilliant opening performance with the Czech Philharmonic Orchestra, but a BBC commentator noted: "The remainder was scuppered by a drifting g-string." Scuppered? Some of us would have paid good money to see that.

Cliff Richard was talking about the trouble he was having topping the pop charts in the Noughties when he chirpily insisted: "I would have No. 2s happily for the rest of my life."

Judy Spiers told Dudley Moore on *Pebble Mill*: "And this is where your career forked off..." No wonder cuddly Dudley collapsed in hysterics!

Chiropodist Brian Berry was talking about ladies shoes on *TVam* when he said: "The sooner women get them off the better." Here, here!

Carl Wilde was talking about a floral display on *This Morning* when he advised Fern Britton: "Make sure your ring's only moist; it won't work if it's soaking wet." Oh, I don't know...

On Richard and Judy's 'You Say, We Pay' section, the female contestant had to make them guess what the picture was in the background behind them. It was a set of bongo drums. "You put it between your legs and bang it!" she told them.

Penny Smith was working out with her personal trainer on *GMTV*. They were demonstrating a back stretching exercise that entailed each of them lifting the other onto their backs in turn. Penny told him: "Now you're going to come on my back."

Post Script

NOT all TV howlers rely on double-meanings of course, and before I leave you, here's a quick round-up of some of my favourite broadcasting blunders that did not involve innuendos. One of the best being the way Ginny Buckley of Sky News brought us word that Harold Pinter had won the Nobel Prize for Literature back in October 2005. She said, and this is verbatim: "Harold Pinter is joining us…the playwright Harold Pinter I believe has just died…news…has just won the Nobel Prize for Literature. Apologies for that…" Dies/prize it's an easy mistake to make.

Then there was the classic BBC News double hand-over when George Alagiah attempted to link back to Natasha Kaplinsky in the studio, saying "It's back to you, Natasha" only for her to come straight back with: "George, thank you. Now it's straight back to Westminster for more of our main story of the day from George Alagiah." Over-reliance on autocues dumbs down presenters, discuss.

BBC newsreader Jonathan Charles gave us another classic in the form of this strange segue into the Josef Fritzl story: "This is BBC World News, I'm Jonathan Charles, kept hidden for more than two years and forced to bear children…" Maybe double check the punctuation next time, mate.

And BBC Breakfast bosses were left red-faced when they broadcast an unedited version of Christian Bale's "You don't fucking understand" tantrum on the set of Terminator Salvation at 6.55am on a weekday morning.

More uncensored swearing came from the US comic Joan Rivers on ITV's cosy day-time show Loose Women. It seems no-one had told her that the programme was live, and Joan gleefully came out with: "Russell Crowe, get ready to bleep this, he is a piece of fucking shit…".

A tongue-tied female presenter on the US shopping channel Atomic Shopping came close. She wanted to say "fitted sheets" but it came out as "This shit…this sheet is fitted." Ah that's a shame, I was after buying the sheeted fits.

THE search for TV howlers goes on. I've just watched the opening episode of this year's I'm A Celebrity…Get Me Out Of Here where the delightful former Page 3 girl Sam Fox informed us "I can feel it coming up" (talking about a crab as she was groping for a star in a bushtucker trial) and "I've only got a little mouth, it's so big!" (talking about an Aussie water spider with three inch legs that she had to hold on her tongue for thirty seconds). This show is guaranteed to deliver rich pickings, I reckon.

Bushell On The Box started in The Sun, enjoyed five years at the People and now appears ever week in the Daily Star Sunday – and I'm still paying £35 for any goof I publish. So buy the paper, and send me any clangers you hear. You might get lucky.

Best wishes

INNUENDO BONANZA!

Garry Bushell

If you like this book, you'll love Garry's new internet-only show

GBH: The Garry Bushell Hour

A Talk Show The Way It Should Be Done: Raw, Honest And Very, Very Funny!

Too risky for radio – and too truthful for television – **GBH: The Garry Bushell Hour** is a new type of show for a new medium.

Litopia.tv/garry

Printed in Great Britain
by Amazon